Connecting
Through
Conversation

Connecting Through Conversation

A Playbook for Talking with Students

Erika Bare
Tiffany Burns

ConnectEDD Publishing
Hanover, Pennsylvania

This publication is available at discount pricing when purchased in quantity for educational purposes, promotions, or fundraisers. For inquiries and details, contact the publisher at: info@connecteddpublishing.com

Published by ConnectEDD Publishing LLC
Hanover, PA
www.connecteddpublishing.com

Cover Design: Kheila Dunkerly

Connecting Through Conversation by Erika Bare and Tiffany Burns. —1st ed.
Paperback ISBN 979-8-9874184-1-3

Praise for *Connecting Through Conversation*

This is a practical guide to support safe and effective conversation and connection between students and the adults who support them at school. The tools and scripts can easily be used by anyone working in education, from support staff to administrators. This playbook is written from the heart by those who live in the education world every day, and the value in that cannot be understated.

—Amy Szeliga | Autism Consultant, BCBA

Connecting Through Conversation: A Playbook for Talking with Students is a must-read for anyone in the field of education. Erika Bare and Tiffany Burns are actually doing the work each day—not studying it from afar. I can't wait to get this book into the hands of our entire school team and to use it as a true playbook to better build meaningful relationships and support students. This is the book we've been waiting for.

—Jennifer K. Parks | K-8 public school principal

Every educator needs to read this book NOW! It both affirmed my focus on good student relationships and gently humbled me to know I have much growth to make. The authors' positivity and love for children bled through every paragraph as well as their support for educators.

—Tara Beals | Elementary Educator

This book is a wonderful compilation of compassionate and respectful strategies for connecting with students in a way that will predictably lead to better behavior management and learning outcomes. Systematic and well-organized, educators of all kinds can use it as a wise guide to tackling specific problems. The examples are down to earth, and the communication strategies are so sensible...and yet would clearly be transformative if they were commonplace. The authors are both experienced educators and school leaders and the book is a manifestation of their commitment to the kind and respectful education of students of all kinds.

—Nando Raynolds, M.A. | Licensed Professional Counselor

Erika Bare and Tiffany Burns know what it means to work with students today. Having worked in the schools for over twenty years, the stressors for students and staff have and will continue to increase. My hope is that through their work in Connecting through Conversation, the transformative experience that is offered in these pages can come to life. When that does happen, it not only comforts and can be healing for the student, but has a ripple effect. Hopefully, this book can serve as a discussion everyday amongst the staff who have chosen to serve students.

—Mary Giancarlo, M.A. | CALC Retired Child Development
    Specialist

Connecting Through Conversation: A Playbook for Talking with Students sparked so many ideas that I had to keep a journal as I went along! My biggest take away: this is not just education reform; this is a structure for a new educational system. A system based in the humanity of self, and our students. I would even venture to suggest that these tools can be used in everyday conversations with acquaintances, friends, colleagues, and family. May this book spark your curiosity and encourage your creativity as it guides you towards more authentic relationships with your students.

—Matthew Reynolds | Human Spirit Amplifier Author of Biggest
    Fullest Brightest: Shifting the Consciousness of Humanity

Finally, a user-friendly, well-informed guide to talking with students. The authors share researched and insightful, yet easy to implement approaches to respectfully conversing with students, even in the most challenging situations. Where these conversations tend to result in win/lose, this book offers the reader an opportunity for a win-win in their work with kids.

—Kim Hosford | School Psychologist

Connecting Through Conversation: A Playbook for Talking with Students is a timely and practical handbook for communicating with students of any age. Keeping connections and relationships at the center of the work, Erika and Tiffany provide immediate, applicable strategies to navigate even the most difficult conversations. This is a must read for all educators!

—Melanie Marrone, Ed.D. | Executive Director, Molalla River
    Academy

Being in a graduate program currently and reading many educational texts at the moment, I can say very honestly that this is as good or better than any I have encountered. The authors explain students' behavior and situations in depth and break them down clearly. They give a bullet point summary of the main points in each chapter, which I love, as a way of recapping the essential information. My favorite thing about this book is that it captures big ideas in classroom management and encourages a positive school culture, but mainly it gives us the essentials of how to interact with young people and uses concrete examples, techniques, and approaches for actively engaging with students.

—Ty Hewitt | Middle School English Teacher and former professor

Connecting Through Conversation demystifies the fundamental process of building powerful relationships between adults and students. Erika and Tiffany do this with profound empathy and a strong equity lens, making these frameworks immediately helpful to educators everywhere.

—Michelle Cummings, Ed.M | Harvard Chief Academic Officer,
    TPT (Teachers Pay Teachers)

"Superb! This is a teacher's book. Burns and Bare have managed to bridge the gap between theory and life in the classroom. Their work is clearly informed by years of excellent practice and shared with an enthusiasm for education that can only come from the best of us."

—Peter Bolling | High School Humanities and AP Government Teacher

Connecting Through Conversation is a must read for educators at all levels. What an encouraging resource for me as I support students in solving problems at school. An easy to read, well-organized play-by-play guidebook for success in building positive relationships with kids. The sentence stems and scenarios are invaluable. I plan to carry this book in my back pocket and have it at the ready!

—Kate Sullivan | Student Advocate, Walker Elementary School Co-director, Ashland Children's Theatre

In their book, *Connecting Through Conversation: A Playbook for Talking with Students*, Erika Bare and Tiffany Burns use their years of experience and knowledge to guide their readers in useful ways to connect with students. Building trusting relationships is often a prerequisite to students learning from educators, and this book teaches the importance and "how to" of just that. I would highly recommend this book to any educator working with children!

—Alex DeSantis | Board Certified Behavior Analyst, M.Ed in Special Education

I enjoyed all the examples and great explanations of how to best help kids while also helping ourselves! There are such amazing resources for brand new teachers to the very experienced educator! It's a great book for any educator to be able to pick up in a multitude of situations!

What a wonderful resource during a new teacher induction or during a professional development!

—Brooke Johnson Thygeson | School Counselor

Connecting Through Conversation is a treasure trove of ideas for any educator. The concepts and strategies in this book can help anyone facilitate successful, empathetic, and engaging conversations. Tiffany and Erika have created an excellent resource for creating a compassionate learning environment through effective communication.

— David Thygeson, 4th Grade Teacher

Erika's Dedication

This book is dedicated to my husband, Tyler, and my two children, Riley and John. I was relieved when my children only laughed a little when I said I was writing a book about how to talk with kids. I am so grateful for the endless learning and growth opportunities they provide me, and the grace they show as we figure it out together. Tyler, thank you for being a partner and supporter in all I do. I love the three of you to the moon and back.

Tiffany's Dedication

To my family—my kind and brilliant, weird and hilarious kids, Harper John and Aven Rosalie, and to their dad, Alec, my love, my partner, my editor, and my best friend. Thank you for your belief and inspiration, your grace and your love. You are magic and my most favorite humans.

Table of Contents

Introduction

*"Connection is why we're here; it is what gives
purpose and meaning to our lives."*

−Brené Brown

D o you talk to kids at school? If so, this book is for you. We wrote this book for all educators. We believe that every adult who talks to students at school is an educator. We work in classrooms, the cafeteria, the office, and on the field. Whether we talk to big kids or little kids, we all have one thing that connects us. We all love children.

If this doesn't resonate with you, we invite you to rethink your career choice. For real. Being an educator requires too many hours for too little pay to do it for any other reason than for the love of children. Adults who have chosen this work belong to the most noble of professions: **Education.**

At the very heart of education is connection.

We wrote this book because we truly believe at the very heart of education is connection. We have witnessed the power of communication transform a moment, a relationship, and a community. Building a culture of connection requires us to communicate with students in a way that shows care, builds relationships, and cultivates learning.

We call the educators who do this well Connected Communicators. In order to have a culture of connection at school, all educators must become Connected Communicators.

When we returned from the years of disrupted learning after the pandemic, we saw clearly that the number of students lagging in social skills, experiencing mental and emotional challenges, and having difficulty communicating their needs in a healthy way had increased exponentially. Anyone who worked with students during this time reported that challenging behaviors occurred at an unprecedented rate. The shared global trauma of COVID-19 had a tremendous impact on our students. At the same time, educators were experiencing the most difficult years of their careers. This created a crisis of culture in our schools. As we emerged from this historic time together, we found ourselves needing to return to the *why* of our work.

Erika and Tiffany became educators many miles apart, both with a genuine desire to make the world a better place. Erika was drawn in by her passion for students with exceptionalities. As she embarked on her career as a special education teacher near Portland, Oregon, she endeavored to provide each student with the individualized supports needed to reach their limitless potential. This has served as the purpose of her work throughout her career as a teacher, coach, assistant principal, building principal, and district administrator. It continues to inspire her today as she learns, laughs, and leads as an assistant superintendent in the same district as Tiffany.

For Tiffany, her own early educational experiences were less than stellar, and provided her with many examples of how *not* to talk to kids. She imagined a school community where students were met with dignity and care. She dreamt of a place where students felt they belonged and knew they were loved. This passion has remained, no matter the role or location. She has taught elementary, middle, and high school students, and worked as an instructional coach, curriculum writer, and university adjunct instructor in Oregon, Alaska, and Mexico. She loves her current role, as an elementary school principal where she is inspired to lead, learn, and play with her favorite people—kids and their grown-ups.

We were lucky enough to connect professionally just over a decade ago as students, writers, and educators in the same administrative licensure program. We were both moms of young children, working as dedicated teachers, when we discovered we had the same vision for education. We were thrilled when we found administrative jobs in the same district. Erika began at a local high school and Tiffany at a nearby elementary school. As we continued to grow together in the profession, we would often share stories, compare notes, and problem solve together.

Reflecting back on our early days of teaching, we both remember finding ourselves in conversations we were not adequately prepared to have. There we suddenly were—social workers, problem solvers, teachers, advisors, and confidants to the children in our charge. As we sought support from our colleagues, we found this struggle was not unique to us. We muddled through, as all educators do, and quickly learned that both *what* you say and *how* you say it matter.

What you say and how you say it matter.

When we became administrators, we felt an urgent need to equip our fellow educators with the skills to communicate with love and respect in every situation. At times, we saw adults talking to children in ways they would never speak to another adult, or in ways they would never wish to be spoken to themselves. We began to wonder what would change if all educators had these communication tools at the ready. What if students felt heard and valued in every exchange they had at school? We searched for a book to help make this possible. We never found it, so we wrote it ourselves.

This book is meant to serve as an easy reference guide, or playbook, if you will, for educators serving students in grades K-12. It is brimming with stories from our forty years of combined experiences in education, as well as some favorites from colleagues we have worked with throughout the years.

The detailed *Table of Contents* is designed to allow you to quickly refer back to an idea, a script, or to review a move as you use them in your practice. In *Part I: Creating a Culture for Connection*, we discuss the foundational concepts that must be in place to build a culture of connection in your school community. This is followed by *Part II: Let Them Catch Your Calm*. In this section, we describe what it takes to get ready for any conversation. In *Part III: Connecting Conversations*, we provide details about how to have conversations so that no learning opportunity for the student is lost. *Part IV: Connecting During the Scary Bits* is all about how to stay connected under pressure, including demystifying common student moves and how to avoid power struggles.

We wrote this book to give educators the tools, strategies, and templates to create a culture of connection in schools. We want to be clear: this is not a system for behavior management. Rather, this is a behavioral approach that will overlay any current discipline system that is trauma informed, culturally responsive, and founded in care for kids. The strategies found in this book will reinvigorate and improve your system, allowing educators to navigate behavioral conversations with both increased confidence and effectiveness.

As grown-ups, we sometimes forget what it is like to be a student. This book will help adults think like students, empathize with their struggles, and use communication to help build and strengthen connection.

Thank you for being an educator. You set the tone and create the culture on the bus, in the lunch line, on the playground, and in the classroom. Thank you for reading this book and beginning the journey to create a culture of connection in schools. We hope you find as much joy and laughter in the reading as we did in the writing.

PART I

Creating a Culture of Connection

"Relationships are as important as the curriculum."

-Zaretta Hammond

CHAPTER 1

Connected Relationships for Learning

"No significant learning occurs without significant relationships."

-Dr. James Comer

Think of the adult in school who made the most positive impact on your learning. Were you able to talk with them? Did you trust them? Did they treat you with dignity? We are going to guess you said, "Yes" to those questions. You're an educator so you know: relationships matter. This concept is not a complex one, but the components of positive relationships can be.

There is an art and a science to building relationships. When we get right down to it, relationships lead to learning when they include the following elements:

Listening → Dignity → Trust = Connected Relationships for Learning

Listening: Hear and Be Here Now

Listening → Dignity → Trust = Connected Relationships for Learning

Students know when we are listening and when we are not. When we are distracted or not giving them our full attention, the message is clear: we aren't listening to them. However, when they have our undivided attention, they talk to us.

When we truly listen, Kids speak their truth.

When we truly listen, kids speak their truth. Not only must we listen, we must also listen *first*. Authentic listening asks us to seek to understand our students before we decide what to do or what to think. When we remain genuinely curious and open, we demonstrate we care, and we show them that what they say matters.

Listening first doesn't build connection if the student does not feel heard. The Connected Communicator demonstrates that a student has been heard and understood by restating, or reflecting back, what the student has said, and then checking to make sure they got it right. Here are some Connecting Through Conversation (CTC) sentence stems you can use to make sure students feel heard.

CTC Sentence Stems to Make Sure Students Feel Heard:

- ◆ "I think I am hearing you say... Did I get that right?"
- ◆ "Let me make sure I have this right..."
- ◆ "Can you help me make sure I understand? Are you saying...?"

When students talk, but don't feel heard, they typically get frustrated. If a student continues to be escalated, they likely do not yet feel understood. We need to better communicate that we are listening and seeking to understand. When students are dysregulated, or in a state of upset, we suggest that you continue to clarify and reframe until the student feels that even if you don't agree, you understand their point of view. Saying, "I hear you" can be a powerful tool to help move the conversation forward, especially when reflecting back what the student actually said.

Students feel heard when we give them our undivided attention, listen first, and explicitly demonstrate that we understand them. When we truly listen to students with an open heart and mind, they share what's on theirs. It is in this listening that we honor students with the dignity they deserve.

> *When we listen to students, we honor them with the dignity they deserve.*

Dignity: Acknowledge Identity to Affirm Dignity

Listening → **Dignity** → Trust = Connected Relationships for Learning

The Connected Communicator ensures that every interaction with kids affirms their inherent dignity. In the book *Belonging Through a Culture of Dignity* by Cobb and Krownapple (2019), the authors share that dignity communicates "the innate, *equal worth* of each human being simply because that person is human. Dignity is our common heritage and birthright as human beings." (p. 95)

Dignity is demonstrated in the way we listen to and treat our students. When we acknowledge their identity, learn their names, pronounce them correctly, and appreciate their unique differences, we affirm their value and worth. We affirm their dignity.

Dignity builds students' sense of belonging in the school community. In *The Gifts of Imperfection*, Brenè Brown (2010) helps us to see the important distinction between belonging and fitting in. "Fitting in is about assessing a situation and becoming who you need to be to be accepted. Belonging, on the other hand, doesn't require us to change who we are; it requires us to be who we are." (p.145) When students' identity is affirmed, they experience belonging, and they feel safe enough to risk learning from us.

Tragically, this affirmation is uncommon for many of our students who do not identify as part of the dominant culture. Our students are all too often asked to assimilate. They are frequently made to give up parts of themselves to fit in. This does not engender dignity. In order to counter this common experience, the Connected Communicator must be explicit and tireless in affirming each student's identity and dignity each day. Zaretta Hammond (2014) shares *In Culturally Responsive Teaching and the Brain* that "Affirming is simply acknowledging the personhood of each student, appreciating all aspects of them, especially those culturally specific traits that have been negated by the dominant culture." (p. 77)

Students who are asked to change who they are so they can fit in do not feel safe. This impacts the brain's ability to learn. As Hammond (2014) tells us, "Trust and fear are inversely related; fear activates the amygdala and the release of cortisol. Cortisol stops all learning for about 20 minutes and stays in the body for up to three hours." (p. 76) Three hours is half a school day of lost learning!

When we know and celebrate our students' unique identities, abilities, backgrounds, learning styles, and cultural heritage, we build a culture of belonging and affirm our students' dignity. Treating each student with dignity creates a safe environment where every student can show up as who they are. When students are accepted as their whole selves, it creates belonging. When students feel a sense of belonging, there is trust.

Trust: Learning is Risky

Listening → Dignity → **Trust** = Connected Relationships for Learning

Learning is an inherently risky and deeply vulnerable endeavor. Think about the last time, as an adult, that you tried to learn something new.

Tiffany recently tried to learn two new sports: skiing and surfing. They were both such humbling experiences, fraught with fear and self-doubt. At times, she got so frustrated, she was tempted to throw her poles into the snow or toss her board into the ocean. The vulnerability necessary to learn these unfamiliar skills provided her perspective, and gifted her a newfound empathy for how students feel every day.

We can all likely remember our first days as educators. It was intimidating, and many of us were plagued with a lack of self-efficacy. Even with this common experience, the risk and vulnerability required to learn something new is an easy thing for us to forget. We tend to expect students to show up to school and learn from us, regardless of the level of trust established. In the *Skillful Teacher*, Stephen Brookfield (2015), as cited in Hammond (2014), shares, "Not trusting teachers has several consequences for students. They are unwilling to submit themselves to the perilous uncertainties of new learning. They avoid risk. They keep their most deeply felt concerns private." (p. 162)

Students take risks every time they learn. It is scary to make mistakes in front of their peers. And yet, we ask them to engage in productive struggle every day. Productive struggle is what happens when we ask students to persevere through new learning and grapple with perplexing concepts. This requires both courage and resolve, and is necessary for true student growth. Students must trust us to learn from us.

Students must trust us to learn from us.

Some students have a harder time building trusting relationships with adults than others. This is especially true for students who have experienced Adverse Childhood Experiences (ACEs). In *Building Resilience in Students Impacted by Adverse Childhood Experiences* by Victoria E. Romero, Ricky Robertson, and Amber Warner (2018), the authors state:

> "Without trust, there can be no authentic relationship with an ACEs student. These young people are adept at reading people. For so many of them, their survival has depended on their ability to read their parents' moods and assess whether a situation is safe . . . Having had experiences that have shattered their trust, these young people can be slow to open up to an adult." (p. 83)

When kids walk into the schoolhouse for the first time, the grown-ups there are strangers and could be unsafe. Until we have built trust, they will be wary of us. Students learn to trust the adults who listen to them, show them care, treat them with dignity, demonstrate integrity, and are consistent and fair.

In a Connected Relationship for Learning, educators must first demonstrate that they are a safe adult who is worthy of their trust. Without it, the vulnerability required for learning is simply too risky an endeavor.

Connecting It: Connected Relationships for Learning

Listening → Dignity → Trust = **Connected Relationships for Learning**

We all understand the significance of relationships. The principles of authentic listening, dignity, and trust create Connected Relationships for Learning. These relationships require connected communication, which is built one conversation at a time. All the tools and strategies found in this book are built upon the foundation that when kids are connected to the educators that serve them, they will learn.

Connected Takeaways

+ When we truly listen, kids speak their truth.
+ Seek to understand before taking action.
+ Acknowledging identity and affirming dignity create a sense of belonging.
+ Dignity builds belonging and safety.
+ Learning is risky and requires trust.
+ Connected relationships are necessary for learning.

CHAPTER 2

Behavior is Communication

"If a kid could do well, he would do well.
Doing well is always preferable to not doing well."

-Ross W. Green

When babies fuss, we know they are not trying to ruin our day. They are telling us something isn't right. They may be hungry, or tired, or uncomfortable. Knowing this, we don't get mad at them, take it personally, or put them in timeout. Instead, we investigate to determine what needs are unmet. Being a parent is often like being a detective. We offer food, we provide extra attention, we put them down for a nap, and we just keep searching until we solve the mystery.

Although older and taller, our students are still not out to ruin our day with their behavior. When students' actions do not align with school expectations, we refer to them as *unexpected behaviors*. This helps us remember that behaviors are not "good" or "bad," they are communication. Connected Communicators know that all behaviors communicate a need or feeling. "In general, human behavior is a complex, ambiguous, and difficult to interpret form of communication. If we are to be successful when working with students. . .we must develop an understanding of the purpose of their behavior." (Romero et al., 2018, p. 6)

All behaviors communicate a need or feeling.

Student behavior is information. By paying attention to what it's telling us, we can use that information to help us identify the need or feeling the student is trying to communicate. Often, students are unaware of their underlying need or feeling. In fact, the behavior expressed is often as much of a surprise to the student as it is to us. As the adults in the room, it is our job to teach students how to name what's going on for them.

It is in this naming that we help students separate the action from their person. The action is not who they are; it is a thing they did. It helps the adult and the child remember that even though what they did was not a good choice, they are still a good kid. Behavior is simply the sharing of a clue, so we can figure out how to meet the need or acknowledge the feeling the student is expressing.

All Behavior Has a Function

Behavior serves a purpose, or function, for the student, whether they know it or not. Helping to identify this function will help both the Connected Communicator and the student. Although the behavior likely has nothing to do with you, your actions will either lead to a Connected Relationship for Learning or a disconnected one that won't.

As a high school principal, Erika was working with a student, who we will call Samantha. Samantha brought alcohol to school, and she was sharing it with several of her friends, hidden in the back hallway of one of the buildings when discovered. This was a student who always did well in school, and had not done anything like this previously. Erika began by investigating why Samantha had made such an unexpected choice in order to determine the important next steps as we describe further in this chapter.

Erika leans on her experience as a special educator when working with all students who make unexpected choices, and did so when working with this student. The roots of using behavioral assessments to determine the function of a behavior originated with special education, and yet these techniques are helpful for all students. Like so many of the techniques special educators use, it is just good practice for all educators. Identifying the function is a critical component to determining next steps, especially if you don't want a repeat performance.

Identify the Function: *Escape, Attention, Tangible Gains, Sensory Needs, or Stimulation* (E.A.T.S.)

Begin your inquiry with the student by asking open-ended questions to start digging into what function a behavior may have been serving for the student. We have included some examples here:

CTC Sentence Stems:

+ "Tell me a little about what happened."
+ "What were you thinking about or feeling when it happened?"
+ "Tell me more about what's going on."
+ "What was going on for you right before that happened?"
+ "What were you hoping would happen?"

A helpful frame when trying to identify the function comes from the organization, *Learning for Justice*. In their publication, *Reframing Classroom Management: A Toolkit for Educators*, Learning for Justice (formerly Teaching Tolerance) provides a plethora of strategies for nurturing positive classroom dynamics. One that we have found particularly useful is the acronym E.A.T.S.: Escape, Attention, Tangible gains, and Sensory needs or Stimulation.

Escape

If a student becomes disruptive right before a subject or activity that is non-preferred, they may be looking to escape. Tiffany worked with a student who showed up to the office daily, but often at different times. When she dug in further, she found that it was always when the class was getting ready to do math. She could expect to see him every day at what the school counselor deemed "math-thirty" until they put an intervention in place. It can help us reframe the escape-seeking behavior when we are sensitive to the reality that students are often more comfortable being seen as a "bad kid" rather than a "dumb kid."

Attention

As Connected Communicators, we prefer to reframe the idea of "attention-seeking" with "connection-seeking." Students could be seeking connection with peers, adults, or both. Think of the student who makes jokes in class at the most challenging times, or is calling out consistently. They may be connection-seeking. This also applies to students who look for any reason in the world to go to the office, even if it means getting kicked out of class for unexpected behavior.

> **CTC Tip:** When students' behavior catches us off-guard, it can be shocking, and you might find yourself at a loss for words. One of our favorite go-to statements is, *"Well, that was unexpected."* This is way better than what we may be thinking, which is often, "What on earth are you doing?!"

When Erika was working with Samantha, she was fortunate to have built a Connected Relationship for Learning previously. She started by asking what happened. Samantha shared that her friends had been leaving her behind at lunch. She didn't think it was on purpose, but she felt lonely and left out. She wanted to do something that she thought would make her more popular with her friends, and guarantee someone to eat with that day. Erika determined this unexpected behavior fell solidly in the connection-seeking category. This is an important distinction, as the more typical response of substance abuse treatment would not address the actual function of the behavior. Instead, Erika decided the intervention needed both a consequence (in accordance with the student handbook) and additional interventions, including social skills instruction and support with friendships.

Tangible Gain

When students display behaviors that offer a tangible gain, the function can be easier to spot. Let's say they grab a toy from a friend, steal something from the teacher's desk, or cheat on a test. They then have the desired item, or score a higher grade on the test. Unexpected behaviors that offer a concrete reward of some kind most often serve the function of tangible gain. In other words, the student is motivated by the outcome, resulting in the unexpected behavior. When the student walks away with a tangible gain, we can deduce this was the purpose, or function of their behavior.

Sensory Needs or Stimulation

Unexpected behaviors that serve the function of meeting sensory needs or stimulation could look like rocking in a chair, tapping a pencil, appearing restless, or other slowly escalating behaviors. Students who are meeting a sensory need are looking for a pleasant sensation or to replace or mitigate some kind of discomfort they are experiencing. (There is much information available on sensory processing and its impact on behavior. If you are interested in diving into this topic further, we encourage you to take a look at *Dunn's Model of Sensory Processing*.)

Each child is unique, and the same behavior from two different kids may be serving very different functions. One may be standing up in the middle of science to gain attention, while another might be seeking to escape the class. One student who is using a substance at school may be struggling with addiction, while, in Smanantha's case, it was connection seeking. To complicate things further, the same behavior could be serving multiple functions at the same time. For example, the student who went to Tiffany's office during math instruction could be seeking connection *and* escaping math. The behavior of leaving math class is the same, but it serves two functions. Because we have built Connected Relationships for Learning, our careful listening, coupled with open-ended questions, will allow us to identify the function for that student. We can then support the student in translating an unexpected behavior into school-appropriate communication.

Examine the Clues: A.B.C.s

Unexpected behaviors are serving a function for a student: they are not about you! Before responding, there are three things we keep central in our minds. First, and perhaps the most important: a student's behavior is what they did, not who they are.

A student's behavior is what they did, not who they are.

Second, behavior is not personal. Finally, they are trying to tell us something. What they are trying to communicate may or may not be clear to us or to the student. In order to figure out what's going on, we need to examine the clues. We use the well-known approach, coined by the grandfather of behaviorism, B.F. Skinner: **A**ntecedent, **B**ehavior, **C**onsequence (A.B.C.). This helps us think through what is happening for the student.

Antecedent

The first clue is to look at what was happening right before the behavior. An antecedent is the thing that happened just prior to the behavior and logically leads to something else happening (think about the whistle to start a race- runners hear the whistle and start running). Another way to think about this is to ask, "What triggered the behavior?" Was the activity changing? Were directions given? Was the class engaged in a task? Was the activity structured or unstructured? Who was around? Was there an audience? Is there disagreement within their peer group? You get the idea. Be looking for clues about what environmental factors or tasks the student was asked to do directly before the behavior. Identifying the antecedents will be critical in prevention down the road.

Behavior

Once you have identified the antecedent(s), think about what the behavior looked like. How would you describe what you saw and heard? How long did it last (duration)? How intense was it? How many times did it occur (frequency)? Was it a new behavior for this student, or one you have seen before? Did the behavior escalate at any point, or was it consistent? The behavior itself is an important clue to determine the function, in particular if we know what consequence the student was looking for.

Consequence

Which leads us to the final step. What was the outcome or consequence for the behavior? The consequences are simply the outcome of any action, and can be positive or negative. For example, if we dedicate ourselves to eating well and exercising regularly, the consequence is improved health. If we stay up way past our bedtime binge watching our favorite show, we are likely to have a really hard time getting out of bed in the morning. In the case of student behavior, the consequence is what happens for the student after the behavior, either positive or negative.

Make the Plan: Prevent, Teach, Reinforce

Now that we have completed the A.B.C.s, it is time to build a plan to support the student. Any student-centered behavior plan should contain three main parts: Prevent, Teach, Reinforce.

Prevent → Teach → Reinforce

We believe that every day is a new day for students, but students are unlikely to have that perspective for adult behavior. Kids expect us to respond today as we did yesterday, if only subconsciously. When they ran out of class yesterday, and they got lots of attention from the grown-ups, they are likely counting on that same consequence the next time. If they told a joke during silent reading yesterday and kids laughed, then there is a good chance that they are looking forward to that same consequence the next day when they tell a joke again.

So when we are thinking about the consequences of the behavior, both positive and negative, is it serving the function the student is after? Let's take a look at a few examples. Let's say Saul loudly shouts out, "This is B.S." when the teacher asks students to hand their assignment to a neighbor to correct. The students all snicker, and the teacher sends Saul into the hall.

Antecedent	Teacher asks students to hand their assignment to a neighbor to correct.
Behavior	Sudden outburst
Consequences	Class laughter
	Student sent into the hall

For Saul, there were two consequences—the class laughed, and Saul was sent into the hall. If he was after peer attention, he got exactly what he was looking for. If he was trying to escape the situation, he got that consequence as well. Either way, the consequences could be inadvertently reinforcing the behavior.

When Erika was at an elementary school, she supported a first-grade student who was consistently running out of the class and heading for the exit. We will call him Jason. When the team ran the behavior through a quick A.B.C. exercise it looked like this:

Antecedent	Asked to work independently, or without adult support
Behavior	Running from the room or activity towards the main exits of the school
Consequence	Time with principal and/or office staff
	A call home to foster parents

As we mapped it out, it became clear that Jason was connection-seeking with adults. We were then freed up to shift to problem-solving about how to stop this from happening in the future. By identifying the antecedent, we were able to be more targeted in our approach. After all, looking at what the function is without using that information to prevent future behaviors is not super helpful.

Prevent

Prevention first! What can you change in the environment? What can be changed about how you are interacting with the student to meet the unmet need, address the skill deficit, or impact the function of the behavior?

Going back to our example of Saul yelling out B.S., we are wondering if there is a less public way to collect homework? Maybe Saul was worried his answers were incorrect and was embarrassed to have a peer correct his paper. We recommend avoiding having peers correct others' work for this reason. Perhaps checking in on progress or answering questions before a public display would help the student feel more comfortable. With Jason, adjusting how we provided positive adult connection throughout class was the first step in prevention. We also arranged a scheduled time during the day that the student could call their foster parent to say hello and give them a status check on their behavior that day.

While we recognize it will take some time on the front end to build a support plan for prevention, we save untold hours of time and angst by putting our energy here.

Teach

Teaching is the next step, and our favorite! After all, it is our job to make sure we teach students the skills needed to appropriately communicate their needs. As Ross W. Greene, PhD shares in his book *Lost at School,* "Figure out what skills he's lacking so you have the clearest possible understanding of what's getting in his way." (2008, p. 10) Dr. Greene's philosophy is that "Kids do well if they can" and is based on the idea that students will do the right thing if they have the skills to do so. It is our job to fill in any skill deficit, so they are equipped to do the right thing. We have been very influenced by Dr. Greene's body of work, and highly recommend Connected Communicators take a deeper dive into his teachings.

Thinking about our example of the student yelling B.S., the teacher might practice using some non-verbal signals with Saul that he can use for a break. They might also privately re-teach Saul ways to get help on an assignment and make some agreements on what is going to work for both him and his teacher. For younger students, giving them the actual words needed is often necessary. We taught Jason to use the phrase, "Can I tell you something?" and used this as a cue for connection. Teaching students an expectation or a replacement behavior requires that we give them the opportunity to practice or rehearse using the skill, just as we do with academic practice.

Reinforce

Once they have learned the skill, reinforce the heck out of it every time they use it. By reinforcing what we want to see more of, we will get more of it. By removing any reinforcement for unexpected behaviors, we should see fewer of those behaviors. For example, if the next day Saul comes to the teacher and asks for help on an assignment, celebrate that. For Jason, the reinforcement of calling his foster parent to share that he had a positive morning at lunch was huge. Our responses, positive and negative, are always reinforcing something for the student. Let's reinforce behaviors that will build connection!

Fair is Not Always Equal

A refrain often heard in the Connected Communicator's classroom is Rick Riordan's lesson from the book *Red Pyramid* , "Fair is not everyone getting the same thing. Fair is everyone getting what they need in order to be successful." (2010, p. 67)Students and adults alike can struggle with this idea. Consider the many learning accommodations educators employ. Often these can be interpreted as "not fair" by students, but as the educator you know you are providing each student the scaffolding they need to be successful. For example, allowing a student extra time on a test or assignment because that student requires additional processing time. Or, having a student work on an extension activity while the rest of the class is still working on a concept that student already has down. The examples are endless. As a special educator, Erika often answered concerns related to "fairness" when implementing accommodations for students. When folks were struggling to understand why it is our obligation to meet each student where they are, she would ask if it is fair for a student in a wheelchair to have access to an elevator, even if the other students don't. The same thinking is required when supporting a student's unexpected behaviors.

Connected Educators are careful to hold the same high expectations for all students, but know consequences are flexible based on the information we have about the individual student. This includes what the student was communicating to us with their behavior, and what function it was serving. Only after these factors have been considered can we design a consequence that is going to maximize the learning opportunity for the student. This leads to different consequences for different students, which can be understandably confusing for kids and the grown-ups who serve them.

For this reason, we need to be intentional in our teaching of fairness versus equality. Early in the school year, we encourage lessons on why fair does not always mean equal. Teachers should provide opportunities for students to think about examples from their own lives, their families, society, or school where this concept applies. The depth of this conversation will vary by age. Rick Riordan's quote can be a great writing prompt, discussion starter, or way to get students thinking about the differences between fair and equal. This applies not only with responding to student behavior, but in how they are supported academically. Thinking about academic differences is often easier than thinking about social emotional differences, and can be a helpful way to start the conversation.

Connected Communicators teach the difference between fairness and equality.

If educators expect that every student will have the same consequence for the same behavior regardless of circumstances, then there is bound to be confusion and frustration. When we are clear that unexpected behaviors will be addressed individually and based on the principles in this book, we will reduce this confusion and frustration. This means consequences may vary depending on the situation. This does not mean we throw out our discipline matrix, but it sets the expectation that all student behaviors will be addressed individually *and* within the context of common expectations.

The students' caregivers also need support in understanding this idea. When discussing their own child's set of circumstances, they are often very invested in knowing what consequences any other students involved received to determine if it was the same or equal. If you've ever been an educator in this situation, you know just how tricky these conversations can be. We have found it is helpful to respond by sharing that we took the situation seriously, each students' behavior was addressed appropriately, and based on what they needed. It is also important to explain that we cannot disclose the details of another student's behavior, in the same way we will not discuss their student's behavior with anyone else.

Connecting It: Behavior is Communication

As Dr. Greene (2008) taught us, "Kids do well if they can." (p. 10) Just as we would not scold a baby for crying when they have no other way to tell us what they need, we need to extend that same grace to our students. Before we say, "Use your words" we need to ensure they have the words necessary to communicate the need or feeling. If students had the words or strategy to communicate appropriately, they would use them. If they aren't using them, then those need to be taught. Communication is a complex skill. It is learned. It is incumbent upon us to teach these skills to our students..

If students had the words to communicate appropriately, they would use them.

When students are behaving in an unexpected way, we can bet there is an unmet need that they are trying to communicate to us. When we take the time to understand the "why" behind the behavior, we can do what we do best, and give them the tools to tell us. Once they have the skills to get their needs met in a positive way, they will use them.

Connected Takeaways

+ All behavior is communication.
+ Behaviors serve a function for the student.
+ A student's behavior is what they did, not who they are.

+ The functions of behavior are Escape, Attention (connection seeking), Tangible gains, and Sensory or Stimulation needs, or E.A.T.S.
+ Commit to memory the phrase, "Well, that was unexpected."
+ Investigate the A.B.C.s (Antecedent, Behavior, and Consequence).
+ Prevent → Teach → Reinforce
+ Once the function is identified, **prevent** the behavior using changes to the environment or educator actions.
+ **Teach** replacement behaviors.
+ **Reinforce** the student when they use appropriate ways to get their needs met.
+ Fair is not equal. Fair is everyone getting what they need.
+ Kids do well when they can.

CHAPTER 3

Emotions are Contagious

"When little people are overwhelmed by big emotions,
it is our job to share our calm, not join their chaos."

-L.R. Knost

You Can't Pour from an Empty Cup

Have you heard the saying "You can't pour from an empty cup"? It relates to the idea that we have to take care of our own needs before we are able to attend to the needs of others. It's fairly obvious when we say it, and yet this struggle is especially common among educators.

We are helpers by nature. We often find ourselves helping our students navigate divorce, loss, abuse, domestic violence, racism, houselessness, and other traumas. When we feel connected to our students and become aware of these traumatic events, we are at risk of experiencing vicarious trauma. This is defined in the article *The Impact of Secondary Trauma on Educators* published on ascd.org "the emotional distress that arises when someone vicariously experiences the traumatic experiences of another individual. Sometimes known as compassion fatigue, the toll of tending to someone's painful experiences can create very real symptoms in caregivers, including teachers." (Baicker, 2020, para. 3). Knowing educators are susceptible to secondary trauma, we must be even more intentional in our efforts to take care of ourselves.

Educators experience great joy with their students, and also stand beside them as they face the saddest of times. The emotionality of our work is undeniable. Many of us have a hard time remembering to take care of our own needs before we try to meet the needs of our students. However, when we do take the time to care for our own body, mind, and emotions, we are less stressed, have more energy, are more creative, have improved happiness levels, and enjoy a host of other benefits. If you are finding it difficult to prioritize yourself, perhaps it would help to reflect on the fact that when we tend to our own well-being, we are more effective. We are better able to serve our students, respond with more care, and show up as our best selves.

> *The emotionality of our work is undeniable.*
> *When we tend to our own*
> *well-being, we are more effective.*

We know that if we are not well physically, emotionally, or mentally, then we cannot be who our students need us to be at school. If our own needs are not attended to, we are trying to pour from an empty cup. This can cause us to be less compassionate or less available to provide support for others. This is especially important when we consider that emotions are contagious.

Emotions are Contagious

Think about a time when you felt another person's energy rub off on you. Imagine your best friend asked you to meet her for dinner to celebrate her new promotion. She spends the meal beaming and enthusiastically sharing the details. You leave the restaurant feeling energized and delighted. You caught her excitement.

Now imagine a family member comes to your home to vent about a maddening exchange he had with one of his friends. His voice is elevated, and he is scowling. As he speaks, he becomes more and more agitated. You find yourself feeling irritated and on edge. You caught his anger.

We have all experienced a contagion of emotions. As it turns out, there is a science behind this. This is our body's way of helping us to empathize and connect with others. This contagion is the result of mirror neurons. According to an article by Lea Winerman (2005) of American Psychological Association, "Mirror neurons are a type of brain cell that responds equally when we perform an action and when we witness someone else perform the same action." Hammond (2014) applies this information to education in her book Culturally Responsive Teaching and the Brain, "To make sure we connect with others, our brains developed mirror neurons to keep in sync with each other. Mirror neurons are special brain cells that prompt us to mimic others." (p. 74) In other words, our mirror neurons respond to the actions and emotions of others. In a sense, humans are hardwired for connection.

Humans are hardwired for connection.

Knowing this, consider whether or not how you are feeling is something you want your students to catch. If not, it is time for a reset. Take a deep breath, have a drink of water, take a break, walk for a few minutes to clear your head—whatever works for you. Just prioritize regulating your emotions. This is important both for you and your students. We want to make sure the emotions students catch from us are positive!

When we consider how transferable emotions are, it is no wonder that educators have to be especially tuned into theirs. This is especially useful when students are demonstrating the opposite of calm.

Let Them Catch Your Calm

Oftentimes when kids are upset, their voice, tone, and rhythm pick up speed and volume. It is surprisingly easy for adults to match a child's patterns of communication without realizing it. This tendency for us to mirror others' behavior is often referred to as the Chameleon Effect as Hattie and Zierer explain in *Mindframes for Visible Learning (2019)*:

> "Interesting in this regard are the studies on the so-called Chameleon Effect. They demonstrate that we unintentionally change our behavior to match that of what we interact with in our social environment, including our posture, casual movements, gestures, facial expressions, and speech tempo to name but a few examples." (p. 137)

Knowing this, we can use this understanding to help regulate students. Instead of rising to a student's emotional state, demonstrate the calm you want them to display. When they are loud and elevated, go lower and slower. Plant your feet firmly on the ground, take a deep breath, and demonstrate the energy you want the student to emulate. When we are able to moderate our voice, tone, and volume, kids are much more likely to do the same.

Make sure the emotions students catch from us are worth catching!

One way to do this explicitly is to use this sentence frame inspired by Jim Fay's *Turn Your Words into Gold* available on Love and Logic website www.loveandlogic.com: "I'll talk to you when your voice is as calm as mine." (Fay, 2023) This models the expectation for students, and signals them to cue into our behavioral state. It also forces us to have a calm and collected tone when we are talking to kids. Can you imagine what it would sound like if we said that phrase using a tone or volume that was anything other than calm? Pretty ridiculous, right?

Tone and Volume

Volume and tone matter. A lot. If we want kids to hear what we are saying, then we need to deliver our messages in ways they can be received. Using a calm tone, and a volume appropriate to the environment allows us to be heard. It also models for the student how we want them to respond. The Crisis Prevention Institute discusses the role of communication at length in their workbook *CPI Nonviolent Crisis Intervention Training* (2020). They state, "Although words are important, the delivery makes the greatest impact on how the message is received." (p. 21)

If, instead, we yell or speak harshly, we are using fear, shame, and intimidation to get students to comply. In the short term, this may get us the result we are looking for, but at what cost? The words of an educator can stay with students for the rest of their lives. Think carefully about the impact of your words before you say them. Additionally, when responding with raised voices or a harsh tone, students are likely to shut down, tune out, or respond with more force. This makes a Connected Conversation unlikely.

> *The words of an educator can stay with students for the rest of their lives.*

Connecting It: Emotions are Contagious

When we use our power to overpower, we are violating the principle of treating all with dignity. Connected Relationships for Learning can be damaged or even broken. When we pay attention to our wellness, recognize the contagious nature of emotions, and model the calm we want our students to feel, we lay the foundation for a Connected Conversation.

Connected Takeaways

+ Educators must attend to their physical, emotional, and mental health.
+ Emotions are contagious—make sure yours are worth catching.
+ When students are elevated, go lower and slower.
+ Our tone and volume matters. A lot.

PART II

Getting Ready for a Connected Conversation

"You are the sky. Everything else—it's just the weather."

-Pema Chodron

CHAPTER 4

Planning a Connected Conversation

"Conversation works for those who work at it."

-John Powell

Through trial, along with some epic errors, we have concluded that when addressing unexpected behavior with a student, a bit of planning can make all the difference. We've found it helpful to use the 4 "Ws" framework to ensure that we are ready. The framework is an examination of *Who* has the conversation, *Where* to hold the conversation, *What* the purpose of the conversation is, and *When* to have it. As we consider these 4 "Ws," we keep the framework of a Connected Relationship for Learning in the front of our thinking. Are the choices we are making upholding the student's dignity? Are we engendering trust? Are we setting up a conversation in such a way that cultivates a Connected Relationship for Learning?

Who

OK, it happened. A student made some unexpected choices, and a conversation is imminent. But *who* should initiate the conversation? Determining who will be most effective in having the conversation is our first decision point, and requires us to ask ourselves some questions. Which adult was the closest to the student when the behavior occurred? Which adult has the strongest relationship with the student? Does the behavior warrant the involvement of an administrator? This step is easy to miss. The times we jumped straight into a conversation without asking ourselves these questions have led to trouble.

Most often, the person closest to the student when the behavior occurred is in the best position to initiate the conversation. If we ask someone else to intervene regarding a behavior that occurred under our supervision, we are telling the student, "This other person is the one who is really in charge, not me." Educators must carefully consider the power they give away when they send a student to the office.

> *Educators must consider carefully the power they give away when they send a student to the office.*

Of course, there are times that help from the office is necessary. Perhaps there is a need for additional privacy, maybe the person with the best relationship *is* in the office, or the situation is serious enough that the support of an administrator is necessary. Once the adult has been identified, it is time to consider the location.

Where

The topic of your conversation should dictate *where* you have it. If frequent informal conversations with students is a part of your daily practice, then you can slide an important conversation into a space that is comfortable and familiar to that student. We encourage all educators to intentionally build these exchanges into their daily routine, regardless of their role.

> **CTC Tip:** Try to engage at least five students in casual conversation each day. Include this in your daily "to do" list both so you remember to do it, and as a reminder that it is not only a fun use of your time, but also a productive one. The more of these casual conversations you've had with a student, the easier it will be to have a difficult one.

If there is a need for a bit more gravity, you can use a space in the office, in the hallway, or in a quiet corner of a classroom. Students who are dysregulated or particularly nervous may need to have the conversation on the move. Some of the most fruitful conversations we've had with students have been while circling the track or swinging side-by-side. Movement is a powerful tool for helping a student regulate after a challenging behavior and for building a Connected Relationship for Learning.

No matter where the conversation takes place, beware of onlookers. We should always consider the level of privacy needed for the conversation. What is the topic of the conversation? What are the potential impacts of the student being seen having the conversation? The answer to these questions will help you determine the location. For example, if you are speaking to the student about something that is private or potentially embarrassing for them, it is important that they are not distracted by who might be able to see or hear them. Privacy is also a consideration when conducting an investigation. If students are aware of who else is being interviewed, it can influence the integrity of the investigation. There are also times when the emotional or physical safety of a witness must be protected.

As an educator, the more you are seen having conversations with students in a variety of places and environments, the more normalized all conversations will be. This will support both the students' privacy and your ability to have the conversations you need to. Besides, what is more fun than talking to kids?

What

When considering the *what* of a conversation, we ask ourselves a few questions. What is the content of the conversation? What needs to be understood or agreed upon by the end of the conversation? Taking a minute to jot down the critical points helps us to clarify our talking points and main ideas. If the conversation is going to have some hard-to-say bits, it is often helpful to have some of your questions or important points you must say written down ahead of time. It gives you a head start on any note taking that is needed, and most importantly, it ensures that you don't forget to ask about a key detail or allow yourself to wiggle out of saying that hard thing.

> **CTC Tip:** Don't go anywhere without your note-taking device and a water bottle! Both can be used as props to provide you or the student some think time. Sometimes being silent is the key for students to figure out a solution rather than us providing it to them.

When

Before selecting the actual time of day, make sure you are prepared for the conversation. An important part of preparation is to ensure you are in the right headspace. Tiffany likes to pay attention to her feet during conversations. When she notices she is resting her weight on her toes, or when her feet begin to climb up her chair leg, she realizes she is less centered. She reminds herself to plant her feet firmly on the floor and secure her grounding.

For Erika it is her heart rate. She will never forget the time she was in a meeting with a student's parents that was not going well at all. As she listened to the parents call her names, promise legal action, and lob a wide variety of insults her way, her Apple Watch started yelling at her too. It began beeping, vibrating, and threatening to call the paramedics on her behalf. Erika frantically attempted to silence the watch while taking some deep breaths to slow her heart rate back to a normal rhythm. While she appreciated her watch's concern, this was a rather embarrassing reminder to take a few deep breaths!

These physical cues remind us to pause and pay attention to what our body is telling us. Take a moment to check in with yourself. Is your heart beating fast? Is your breathing shallow? Are your thoughts racing? Where are your feet? If your body is telling you that you are not ready, take a moment and regulate. Have a drink of water, take some deep breaths, count backwards from twenty. Still feeling heightened? Push pause on the conversation.

> **CTC Tip:** Lean on your team. Not all educators are responsible for supervising a classroom at all times. Arrange for staff members who are available to respond to a text or phone call to cover for a teacher when they need five minutes. There is magic in being able to take a quick walk to recenter. Identify who is on call for such breaks at what times and encourage educators to take a minute when they need it.

To determine if you are ready to have a Connected Conversation, ask yourself some questions about how you are feeling emotionally. Are you angry? Are you scared? Are you hurt? If the answers to any of these questions are yes, you've got some reflecting to do. Connected Communicators take the time to understand their own triggers, and analyze why they are being impacted in such a personal way. Try as you might not to take things personally, you are still a person. Do what you can to separate the behavior from the student, and don't dive in until you are certain that your emotions won't take over.

Even when it isn't personal, an educator is still a person.

Now that you know you are ready, the actual time can be dictated for you by the daily schedule and the urgency of the conversation. When you have the benefit of flexibility, think strategically about what part of the day works best. If the conversation is likely to make learning difficult for the rest of the day, avoid having the conversation first thing. If the student is anticipating the conversation, and will be distracted until it takes place, have it as soon as possible. Even though they did something that requires a difficult conversation, students are here to learn. We respect their dignity by reducing the impact on their learning as much as possible.

If you are trying to keep the conversation casual, time your conversation in a way that might occur naturally on the playground or during a passing period. Meeting in a natural way reduces the student's level of concern as opposed to sending a note or calling a student out of class. If the conversation is going to take some time, avoid having it at a time the student is going to be anxious to return to their favorite period of the day (lunch, P.E., and so on).

Do your best to estimate the amount of time needed for the conversation, and make sure you allow yourself enough time to have it. You may also consider breaking a conversation up into parts if you want the student to have some additional think time, or if you need to gather more information based on what you hear.

Connecting It: Planning a Connected Conversation

The *Who, Where, What,* and *When* of a conversation can make or break connection. While it might be tempting to skimp on the preparation in order to save time, it almost always costs us more time in the end to clean up any mess made when we have the conversation before we are ready. We have included a Connected Conversation Planning Guide Template in the appendix as a tool.

Connected Takeaways

+ Behavioral conversations are usually best had by those who were closest to the student when the behavior occurred.
+ Carefully consider the power you give away when you send a student to the office.
+ Consider location factors: privacy, gravity, and student comfort.
+ Utilize the Connected Conversation Planning Guide in the appendix to prepare for the conversation.
+ Plan your talking points in advance, and be clear on the purpose.
+ Have the conversation at a time of day least likely to impact learning and allow you enough time.
+ Be emotionally and mentally regulated before beginning the conversation.

CHAPTER 5

Care Out Loud

"People don't care how much you know
until they know how much you care."

-often attributed to Theodore Roosevelt

Kids need to know that we care about them. How do we make sure they know? We tell them. Out loud. This is precisely what we mean when we say Care Out Loud. Although it is true that actions speak louder than words, when it comes to expressing care, we need to both demonstrate our care through our actions, and explicitly say it as often as possible. Hearing that you are loved and cared for never gets old, and only serves to support building Connected Relationships for Learning.

Say It Out Loud

Connected Communicators build these statements into their daily routines and interactions as frequently as possible. Here are some simple ways to tell students you care about them. It is important to be authentic, so only use what works for you.

+ I care about you.
+ You're awesome!
+ I'm so glad you are here.
+ This class is better because you are in it.
+ Your success is important to me, because you are important to me.
+ You matter.
+ You're a rock star!
+ You have so much to be proud of!
+ I am so glad you are in this class/on this bus/on this team/at our school.
+ You are such a cool kid!

You get the idea. We don't always know how much students need to hear from a respected grown-up that they are loved and cared for. Find some phrases that work for you, and make sure to say them out loud regularly. Connected Communicators want to know that each kid is hearing how special they are with enough frequency that they internalize the message.

Show Care with Action

We have all heard that actions speak louder than words. We don't disagree, and when it comes to supporting students, explicitly *stating* we care should be accompanied by explicitly *showing* we care. There are several easy techniques that we have built into our routines to demonstrate care:

Intentionally greet each student when they arrive: This can be as simple as greeting students with a smile and saying, "Hi Jamar, I am so glad to see you today." If you can be near the bus loop, or in the hallway in front of the classroom to welcome students as they arrive, do it. If you are the bus driver, you are setting the tone for the day. This serves more than one purpose. Students feel valued when we greet them by name, and we notice that we feel more connected all day long.

Say an individual goodbye as students leave: Taking the time to end with a positive exchange can make all the difference. The first and last things we hear stick with us the longest. Take advantage of this by using this time to remind students you care about them. Student pick up areas are great places to build relationships with students and their families. Get out there and say goodbye.

Get to know students using writing or interviewing: Many teachers have students write a letter introducing themselves to the teacher, or some version of this at the start of the year. With younger students, using interviews, surveys, or drawings can also be effective ways to get to know them right away. Consider the following writing or interview prompts:

- What is something you would like me to know about you?
- Tell me about the people you live with.
- What helps you learn best?
- What are you good at? What's hard for you?

Keep the conversation going: When we ask students to write to us, we make sure to write back. This is a great opportunity to provide personalized feedback on what makes them awesome. Make as many connections as you can to what they shared about themselves. For example, "It is so cool that you like to swim; I have always loved to be in the water." You might want to develop a system for keeping track of these tidbits so you can refer to them later when you need to break the ice.

Provide meaningful praise on their work and their progress: Sharing with them how impressed you are of their growth and accomplishments will fill students with pride. This will also make it more likely they'll keep it up.

Celebrate their birthdays—no matter how old they are: We are never too old to appreciate being wished a happy birthday. Before the year starts, make sure each student's birthday is calendared, either publicly or on your own calendar, and establish a birthday tradition. In the classroom, maybe the student gets a small prize, and the class sings happy birthday. Maybe the birthday student selects part of the lesson for that day. Maybe you all get a small treat. At the school level, share birthdays over the loudspeaker, have a monthly birthday lunch bunch, or send a positive note home to the birthday student's family. If you have a digital reader board, add birthday students to the running announcements. Whatever it is, the key piece is to acknowledge their special day, and let them know we are glad they were born.

Give them choice and ownership in their education: Wherever we can provide students choice, we should. Are there different ways to demonstrate their learning for a particular standard? Could there be a vote on an important decision for the class or school? What if the class works together to establish classroom agreements? How could a school administrator or teacher use classroom circles to gather information about an important decision? This is their education, and we want them to know it belongs to them.

This is their education, and we want them to know it belongs to them.

Ask for feedback and use it: When we ask students for feedback, it lets them know we care what they think because we honor and respect them. Get feedback early and often, and share with them how you will use it. This means you need the information *before* the school year ends.

COLBA: Care Out Loud Behavioral Approach

Caring Out Loud becomes even more impactful when supporting a student after an unexpected behavior. As we discussed in a previous chapter, *Behavior is Communication*, separating the child from the behavior is critical for students' sense of self.

Tiffany starts almost all conversations in her office related to behavior with some version of, "I know you are a good kid. Sometimes even really good kids make mistakes." This immediately tells the student that they are known and cared for. It also explicitly states that our care for the student is not lessened based on what they did. The impact of this powerful tool can be seen in the students' shift in demeanor and how they engage in the conversation. We call this strategy for building a Connected Relationships for Learning the **Care Out Loud Behavior Approach**, or COLBA.

COLBA:
I know you are a good kid. Sometimes even really good kids make mistakes.

When students have engaged in unexpected behavior, they are going to assume you are mad at them. That is a natural conclusion, and is likely based on past experience with adults. This makes it all the more critical that we assure them that we are not addressing the unexpected behavior because we are angry. We are addressing it to teach them and keep the school safe for everyone.

If the student worries that you are mad at them, your response is important. The answer when they ask is always no. Remember, whatever just happened is not about you. Get on their level and say very clearly, "I'm not mad at you. I care about you. And we need to talk about this situation."

> **CTC Tip:** Kids know if we are telling the truth, so you'll need to mean this when you say it. If you are actually mad, you know what to do. Wait until you are ready to talk.

Once they have been assured that you are not mad, you can begin talking about the unexpected behavior you are addressing in the conversation. This is why starting the conversation with a version of COLBA is such a powerful strategy.

Now that you have established that you hold them in high esteem, you can transition into helping them with what to do next. We like to say something like, "The most important thing when we make a mistake is to own up and take responsibility." It might sound like this:

> **Connected Communicator:** "Malcolm, I need to talk with you about what happened on the playground earlier today. You are such a great kid, and I think it is important for you to know that even great kids make mistakes sometimes. Even great grown-ups make mistakes! The most important thing to do when that happens is to take responsibility for your actions and do what we can to make it right. What do you want to tell me about what happened?

This start to the conversation lays the groundwork for a Connected Conversation. Notice the Connected Communicator's use of COLBA.

This does a number of things. First, the adult has made it clear they care about the student. Second, they have separated *what* the student did from *who* that student is. Finally, they gave clear direction to the student as to what is important now. It also encourages the student to be honest and forthcoming about what actually occurred. Of course, this does not guarantee the conversation will be a total success, but the proper foundation has been laid.

How we end these conversations is as important as how we start them. If the students took accountability and processed with you, then tell them how proud they should be of themselves. Acknowledge how much courage it takes to tell the truth, and that you admire them for that. If they apologized, made a repair, and made assurances that they will not repeat the behavior, give them lots of praise for taking accountability, and let them know how much you look forward to hearing how they followed through.

When they have made a mistake, it becomes all the more critical to assure them that our care for them is not diminished. This is an especially important time to Care Out Loud. They need to know that your Connected Relationship for Learning is not broken.

> *When a child has made a mistake, it becomes all the more critical to Care Out Loud.*

Connecting It: Care Out Loud

No matter what a student's world looks like outside of school, Connected Communicators ensure that every single kid who steps into our schoolhouse knows they are loved and cared for. They know this because they hear it—every single day. They hear it because we Care Out Loud. They see it, because we practice daily routines that show care. They know it, because we say it and demonstrate it frequently enough for them to internalize it. We want to be that person the student remembers years after they have graduated. We want them to remember us because of how we made them feel.

Connected Takeaways

+ Students need to hear and see how much we care about them so this can be internalized.
+ Tell kids frequently and intentionally how much you care for and appreciate them.
+ Use regular routines to show students how much you care about them.
+ Caring Out Loud is especially important when addressing unexpected behaviors.
+ Care Out Loud Behavioral Approach (COLBA): You're a really good kid, sometimes even really good kids make mistakes.

CHAPTER 6

Small Talk Isn't Small

"Small talk is the biggest talk we do."

-Susan RoAne

S mall talk may seem small, but can be huge when used well. It can help a child feel comfortable chatting with you before diving into deeper topics. The more often we engage in low-stakes conversations with our students, the more comfortable and easy the high-stakes conversation is going to be. After all, this is how Connected Relationships for Learning are built. We need to talk to each other to get to know one another.

The More You Know

The Connected Communicator gets to know their students. We are collecting information all the time. Do they have siblings? Do they play sports? What video game do they like? Is there a show or a band they are into? As you learn these important bits of information about your students, be sure to file them away. It will make any subsequent conversation so much easier.

Remembering something you discussed with a student days or weeks earlier demonstrates care and shows students that you are paying attention to who they are. The more kids you work with, the harder it is to keep track. Erika went so far as to write down what she learned about her students and stored this information in a binder she kept by her desk.

CTC Tip: Gathering information via a survey, or a "getting to know you assignment" about interests and preferences can be a great way to build up your bank of information.

In a pinch, having some conversation stems in your back pocket can be so helpful. Here are just a few:

CTC Sentence Stems for Younger Students:

- What's your favorite part of the day?
- If you could wish for three things what would they be?
- What is something that cheers you up when you are sad?
- What do you think is the best part of being a grown-up? Being a kid?
- If you could eat only one food for the rest of your life, what would it be?
- If you had a magic wand, what is the first thing you would do with it?
- What is something you are really good at?
- What is the funniest joke you know?

CTC Sentence Stems for Older Students:

- What is your favorite after school activity? What do you like about it?

+ What school rule do you wish would be eliminated? Why?
+ What are you most proud of?
+ What kind of movies do you like to watch? Why?
+ If you had to pick just one cause to fight for, which one would it be?
+ What advice would you give to adults about how to make the world a better place by the time you are an adult?
+ What is most exciting about what comes after high school?
+ What do you find most stressful about it?
+ What advice do you have for students getting ready to start at the high school/middle school?

In addition to knowing our students, knowing their families can make all the difference. When we invest in building relationships with the important people in a student's life, we help strengthen the bond with the student and contribute to a culture of connection at school. When educators make connections with a student's family, it builds stronger bonds at school.

Break the Ice

Of course, we do not always have the luxury of getting to know a student well before an important conversation. Before diving in, we recommend engaging in low-stakes dialogue. This doesn't have to be complicated. Start with the obvious things. Look at what they are wearing. Does their shirt or hat have a sports team, animal, or other design that you can ask about? Has there been a recent school activity that you can talk about? Ask them if they went to homecoming, or if they plan to attend the upcoming basketball game.

Keep your finger on the pulse of current cultural trends for the students you serve, and be careful not to trivialize these. Cultural trends make a generation who they are.

Cultural trends make a generation who they are.

Erika used to make pop culture a regular agenda item when she met with the Student Body Presidents at the high school where she worked. The school included the music, social media platforms, and influential voices of the time into school-wide culture by infusing them into assemblies, sporting events, dances, school communications, etc.

> **CTC Tip:** Ask about the most recent viral trend or video game. You don't have to play or even watch to know enough to ask. Get a quick lesson from your own child, or a niece or nephew.

Sharing Yourself

Another technique to get the conversational ball rolling is to share something about yourself. This is especially useful when the student appears reluctant to share much. Talk to them about your favorites, share a silly anecdote about a pet, offer a funny story about yourself or your family. Tiffany often shares humorous anecdotes from her own adventures in elementary school when talking with students. Erika likes to talk about her first job dressing up as the Mouse at Chuck E Cheese, or a story about her very entertaining cat. Each of us has a unique life experience. Our personal stories, so long as they don't cross a privacy line, provide a wealth of genuine ways to get the conversation started.

Being vulnerable in this way humanizes you which, in turn, leads to building Connected Relationships for Learning. You can use these anecdotes to get them talking. When a student has the opportunity to get to know you better, there is an increased level of trust and care between you and the student. When kids feel they know you and you know them, they see you care. And that helps them care about you. They now are going to be more invested in your Connected Relationship for Learning.

When the Ice Won't Thaw

Sometimes all attempts at small talk seem to be in vain. In Erika's first year of teaching, she struggled to make conversation with a student we will call David. This student experienced autism and was very, very interested in airplanes. She pulled out all the usual tricks, focusing on his areas of interest and sharing what she thought were hysterical stories about her cat. She asked him about airplanes, his classes, his day. In most attempts, she would get no more than a one or two-word response. Sometimes there was no response at all.

It was important to thaw this very stubborn ice for this particular student. First, Erika knew how critical a Connected Relationship for Learning was for David. Second, David struggled with some unexpected behaviors, necessitating a number of higher-stakes conversations. She ended up compiling everything she knew about David and made a plan.

During a lunch period one day, she set out to find David. She found him in his usual spot, sitting on the floor in the back corner of the library with his back against the wall. She slid down next to him and didn't say anything for a few moments. Finally, staring straight ahead, she said, "David, I am wondering if you would be willing to give me a lesson in the difference between passenger planes and fighter jets." He looked down at his watch, paused, and announced that he couldn't teach her everything because he only had eight minutes before the next class began. He said more in those eight minutes than he had all year. Every conversation after that came easier.

Once you've had a Connected Conversation, every conversation after that becomes easier.

For this to work, it had to be intentional. Erika selected an environment she knew would be quiet with limited visual stimuli. She was sitting at his level next to him, not facing him. She also made sure he got to set the terms of the length of the conversation. Finally, the question was not only in an area of interest, but also open-ended.

The critical thing is to not stop trying. Some students are harder to get to know than others. You may have to use up every one of your great stories, and try a seemingly endless number of conversation starters. With time and effort, you will thaw the ice, and it will be worth it. Erika saw the impact of this at graduation when David's mom gave her a huge hug and thanked her for knowing her son. One connected conversation in sixth grade made a difference for David and his family.

Connecting It: Small Talk Isn't Small

Engaging in frequent small talk with students is going to humanize you, help you to get to know your students better, and improve the culture of your school. It is especially helpful to start with something small before diving into something big. If you are escorting a student somewhere to have a big talk, use the journey to have a little talk to lay the foundation. If you can get them to smile or laugh prior to the bigger conversation, all the better. The important thing is to make sure the ice is good and thawed for everyone involved before diving in.

Connected Takeaways

+ Take time to learn about your students' interests and lives outside of school.

+ Develop a system to remember what you learn.
+ Get to know the important people in each student's life.
+ Have a few conversation stems in your back pocket.
+ Stay current on the latest cultural trends
+ Share fun or interesting information about yourself
+ When you are consistently struggling to engage a particular student in conversation, be intentional in your approach and don't give up.
+ Always make sure the ice is good and thawed before diving into a higher-stakes conversation.

CHAPTER 7

To Talk or Not to Talk

"Listen to Silence. It has so much to say."

-Rumi

C an you remember a time when you were quite upset? Maybe you were crying uncontrollably or perhaps visibly angry or frustrated. Can you remember how you felt in your body? Now, can you imagine how you might respond if an authority figure intervened with directions or criticism? What if they tried to direct your tone or volume? Or what if they told you to calm down or relax? What if they reminded you that your behavior was uncalled for and asked you to think about a more appropriate response to the situation? In our experience, these common responses tend to further escalate any individual.

When adults are upset, angry, or near tears, we need time. We need a minute to catch our breath, regulate, and get back into our bodies. Kids need the *exact same thing*. Sometimes they might need help getting calm; however, when a child is having a tantrum, screaming, crying, or acting out physically, it is impossible to engage in a Connected Conversation.

Wait!

Silent wait time can be our friend here. It isn't just for classroom lessons, and while it may not feel natural at first, it is a useful tool to help students become regulated. In fact, any noise at all can have a negative effect on a student's ability to think. According to Daniel Gross in his article, *"This is your Brain on Silence,* published on *nautil.us,* "Noises first activate the amygdala, clusters of neurons located in the temporal lobes of the brain, associated with memory formation and emotions. The activation prompts an immediate release of stress hormones like cortisol." (Gross, 2014, para. 11) When students are already in a heightened state of distress, we are trying to decrease their stress level, not add to it!

When remaining silent with a student, you might consider modeling some calming strategies. Take some deep breaths. They may decide to breathe with you. Take a moment and get a drink of water and offer them one as well. Kids, like adults, need opportunities to think uninterrupted thoughts.

> ## *Kids, like adults, need opportunities to think uninterrupted thoughts.*

If, after this wait time they continue to be escalated, they are telling you, "I'm not ready. I need more time." Gift them this. For younger students you might try setting a timer and letting them know that you will be back to see if they are ready to talk when it goes off.

As much as we want students to be on our timeline, they are not. We can't rush de-escalation, so we shouldn't rush the conversation. When we try to hurry them along, it typically takes us even longer to engage them in a Connected Conversation.

De-Escalate

These strategies give students (and their grown-ups) time to breathe, pause, think, and de-escalate. Once students are calm, they are able to receive the information you wish to share, and you stand a much better chance of having a successful conversation:

CTC Tip: When Students are Escalated, *try* this:
   + Offer a fidget toy.
   + Provide a weighted lap blanket.
   + Model deep breathing, and invite the student to join you.
   + Give the student some water.
   + Take a walk.
   + Use distraction with younger students.

CTC Tip: When Students are Escalated, *avoid* this:
   + Telling the student to calm down.
   + Asking them to write about their behavior.
   + Telling them to think about what just happened.
   + Threatening possible consequences for their behavior.
   + Interrupting the student if they are talking.
   + Using too many words.
   + Beginning to process or debrief the behavior.

Move

Sometimes, it helps to allow students an opportunity to move their bodies. One of Tiffany's favorite strategies (when she is not concerned about the possibility of a child fleeing), is to go on a walk with them. While they are walking around campus, she gives the student as much choice as possible with which path to take, where to turn, and when to turn back. This strategy gives the student an opportunity to calm down and be ready to talk. Tiffany takes the students' lead so sometimes they walk in silence and other times they engage in small talk. She pays attention to the student's cues to see when they are ready to transition to a Connected Conversation.

You might also consider transitioning to a new location. Moving from one place to another can be calming in and of itself. Giving them a pathway for distraction through movement can be a welcome gift. For example, saying to a student, "I can see you are really upset. Maybe we could go play basketball for a bit to take our minds off things for a few minutes." When you play basketball, just play basketball. Let go of the expectation of conversation until it is clear they are ready.

Ready; Not Ready

We often find ourselves employing a technique we learned from behavioral psychologist Timothy J. Feeney, PhD, who has worked supporting students with behavioral challenges in schools throughout the U.S. He offers what we have found to be a very effective strategy to share with students when they are acting out. He suggests that adults give students something physical and observable to do to demonstrate they are "ready." The adult is then able to easily observe the student complete a basic physical task, which indicates they are ready. This reduces the pressure for the student or adult to engage verbally before the student is ready, which could escalate the behavior. You might say to escalated students, "I can see you are not ready. I'll know you are ready when you (insert motor movement here)." For example:

+ I'll know you are ready when you sit in your chair and pick up your pencil.
+ I'll know you are ready when you open your book to page 32.
+ I'll know you are ready when you join us on the carpet.

If you come back to them and they haven't done the motor movement yet, simply say, "Oh. It looks like you are not ready. I will know you are ready when (restate the motor movement prompt)." When they are ready and do the motor movement, you can say, "Great, it looks like you are ready."

This same strategy can apply when students are really upset. When a student is escalated, you might say, "I can see you are not ready to talk about what happened. I will know you are ready when you are able to move into this chair so we can talk," or "I can see you are not ready to talk with Ms. Stewart. I will know you are ready when you lift your head up off your desk." By acknowledging they are not ready, and then giving them a physical task to do to cue you when they are ready, it allows the student some choice and an opportunity to take the time they need. While you are waiting for the student to be ready, remain quiet.

Take, for example, Martin, a 7th grade student in the script below. Martin is refusing to engage in his writing assessment. He shoves his papers off his desk and breaks his pencil. He yells, "This is child abuse! I'm not doing your stupid test." He then pulls up the hood on his sweatshirt and puts his head down on the table.

> **Teacher** (leaning down next to Martin and in a quiet voice): Martin, it seems like you are frustrated. I'd like to help, but I can see you are not ready to talk. I'll know you're ready when you lift your head up off your desk.
> **Martin** (mumbling from under his hood): Whatever.
> **Teacher** (in a neutral voice): OK. I'll come back when I see you're ready to talk because your head is up.
> (Teacher circulates around the class, checking in with other students. Martin still has his head down.)

Teacher (returning to Martin a few minutes later): Martin, just checking to see if you are ready to talk. I'll know you are ready when your head is up.

(Martin does not reply and does not sit up. Teacher leaves again and assists other students. A few minutes later, the teacher notices that Martin's head is up. Teacher walks to Martin.)

Teacher: It looks like you are ready to talk. Tell me about what's going on.

Notice how the teacher used very few words to communicate and did not ask questions. The teacher employed the broken record technique by using consistent language over and over. The teacher was clear with his expectation and showed care by saying he wanted to help. He did not apply pressure or confront Martin about his behavior while he was escalated. Of course, the teacher will address the behavior now that Martin is no longer escalated and demonstrating that he is ready for a Connected Conversation.

When kids are escalated, stop talking.

Connecting It: To Talk or Not to Talk

While we know this sounds straightforward, we cannot count how many times we have seen well-intentioned adults attempt to debrief a situation or rationalize with a child when the student is still escalated. We've been guilty of this ourselves. However, we know that when we try to talk to kids when they are still escalated, it simply doesn't work. Stop talking and wait it out.

Connected Takeaways:

- When kids are escalated, stop talking.
- Trying to rush a conversation before a child is de-escalated doesn't work.
- Resist the urge to push the child to be on your timeline. The more you push them to be ready to talk, the longer it will take.
- Use the Ready, Not Ready technique when students are acting out or are escalated.

CHAPTER 8

Your Body is Talking.
What's it Saying?

"Your body communicates as well as your mouth.
Don't contradict yourself."

-Allen Ruddock

The way in which we hold our body sends messages, intended or not, to our students. It lets students know if you are feeling confident or insecure, angry, or open. You may have heard of the seven percent rule, shared way back in 1971 by Albert Mehrabian. He claimed in his book *Silent Messages* (1971) that 7% of meaning comes from the words we say, 38% through our tone of voice, and 55% through body language. This means that more than half of our communication is non-verbal so we better pay attention to what our bodies are saying.

Kids are more likely to engage with a grown-up who has an open posture and is smiling, than a grown-up with their arms crossed and scowling. Can you blame them? And yet, you may not even be aware of what your body is saying. Unless you are paying attention, you may not realize your resting face might look a bit, let's say, grumpy. If that is the case for you, like it is for Erika, you must consciously put a smile on.

Get on Their Level

Those in the corporate world know how to use body positioning to communicate a position of power. They might stand while others are seated, or position themselves behind a large desk. We have all been in the situation of talking to someone while we are seated and the other person is standing. Does it have an impact on how comfortable you feel? Typically, the increased power difference that occurs when using this type of body language negatively impacts communication. This is especially true at school with the inherent power differential that exists between children and adults. Add in the physical differences in height between younger children and grown-ups, and it is downright intimidating.

Knowing this, anytime you can get on the same level as a child when having a one-on-one conversation, do so. If they are in a chair, can you sit next to them? If they are standing, can you squat or bend down? The same is true when talking to a small group of students. Being on the same level reduces the power differential, and it shows them that you are not above them–physically or figuratively.

Being on the same level reduces the power differential. It shows students you are not above them- physically or figuratively.

Remove Barriers

It does not foster connection when we place a power object, like a desk, between us and a student. We know you do not often have the opportunity to sit at your desk while students are in the room, but in the rare instance you do, make sure that any student who comes up to talk to you is able to sit next to you, as opposed to on the other side of the desk. If you are the principal, move yourself to a conference table or to a pair of chairs next to each other when you are talking to a student (or another educator for that matter). Removal of this barrier allows for an open posture, and lowers the power differential that exists.

Side-by-Side is Best

When talking with a student one-on-one, it is typically best to be side-by-side, or at a roughly ninety-degree angle as opposed to face-to-face. When we square our shoulders to someone, it unconsciously conveys dominance, and can be perceived as threatening. It also forces eye contact, which we generally discourage. Read more about that in our Chapter *To Look or Not to Look*. If you are a parent, you may have noticed that your own kids suddenly start sharing during car rides. Being seated side-by-side with no expectation of eye contact takes the pressure off, and the flood gates can open.

How you position your body in relation to the student is especially important when discussing a difficult topic, or helping them process their actions or feelings. Take a chair and slide it next to the student, or lean on the wall next to them in the hall. When we position ourselves next to students, side-by-side, without barriers between us, it immediately makes us more accessible. If the student is especially escalated, the safest stance according to the Crisis Prevention Institute (crisisprevention.com) for you and the student is to be at roughly a ninety-degree angle from the student with one foot about eighteen inches behind the other. This allows you to be in a supportive posture, while providing physical stability and the ability to move quickly if necessary.

CPI Stance

Credit: Alec Dickinson

What To Do with Your Hands

Beyond physical position, you will also want to think about what your hands are doing. Are they on your hips? Are they pointing? If so, you'll likely want to change that. Our bodies should say, "You can talk to me. I want to help you, not boss you." You can picture it, right? The well-intentioned adult towering over a child with one hand on their hip and one finger wagging away? They are doing something out loud, and it's certainly not communicating care.

Tiffany recalls a time when she was walking down the hallway, and could see from a distance an adult standing over a student with their finger pointing at them. She could not hear what was said, but could see damage was being done to the relationship. Upon learning more, the situation the teacher was attempting to address could have been easily solved if her body was saying the same thing her words were. Instead, the teacher needed some coaching to repair the relationship that was harmed. In the conversation Tiffany had with the teacher, it became clear that the teacher was unaware of what their body was saying.

Connected Communicators are mindful of what their hands are saying. Another stance to avoid is having your arms crossed. Erika learned a valuable lesson about that resting grumpy face and how to deal with cold temperatures when outside during a passing period at the high school. A student who she knows well came up and said, "What's wrong? Who are you mad at?" Truth was, Erika was crossing her arms to keep herself warm, while also thinking about a meeting she was headed into after the passing period. Then forward, she learned to always wear a smile when not alone in her office. And to wear lots of layers!

You can also use your hands to offer support. Putting your hand on a student's arm or shoulder when they are upset or sharing something hard shows care and concern. If physically touching the student is not appropriate, you can also convey this by placing your hand on your heart while they are talking.

Connecting It: Your Body is Talking

The experts tell us anywhere from 70% to 90% of what a person communicates is non-verbal (Mehrabian, 1971). We know this, and yet we don't always stop to consider what our body is saying. When we are mindful of our non-verbal communication, the messages our bodies send become tools for Connected Relationships for Learning. Get on their level, position yourself side-by-side or at an angle, and remove any barriers. Make sure your hands are conveying care. Remember, if your *body* is positioned to not look scary, *you* don't look scary.

Connected Takeaways

+ Body Language makes up *at least* 55% of what is communicated (Mehrabian, 1971).
+ Be aware of your resting face.
+ Get on the students' level whenever possible.
+ Position yourself side-by-side or at an angle.
+ Use your hands to convey care.

CHAPTER 9

To Look or Not to Look

"When I look at someone straight in the eye, I feel as if their eyes are burning me and I really feel as if I am looking into the face of an alien. I know it sounds rude but I am telling it how it is."

-Luke Jackson, an author who identifies
as being on the autism spectrum

People have strong feelings about eye contact. We cannot count how many times we have heard the phrase, "Look at me when I am talking to you." Ask yourself: How does this statement resonate for you? Does it engender connection? Does this make you want to engage with the person making this demand? For many kids and adults, eye contact can be threatening, stressful, and even scary.

Think back to a time you were on the receiving end of a difficult conversation. Was it super comfy for you to look directly into the eyes of the other person? Were you able to hold eye contact the entire time? Or did you need to look away to really listen to what the person was telling you? Hearing criticism or critique is challenging–no matter how gently or compassionately it is delivered. When we want kids to hear what we are saying and reflect in order to make different choices moving forward, we need to help them feel super comfy.

Eye Contact is Individually, Situationally, and Culturally Specific

The psychology of eye contact is complicated. An individual's life experiences, neurology, and culture can drastically impact their use of, and comfort with, eye contact. Depending on the situation, a student could have varying levels of comfort with direct eye contact. If they are excited and wanting to share their enthusiasm with you, they might be very comfortable using eye contact. If they are feeling nervous or threatened, they may not engage in any direct eye contact at all. Importantly, students who experience neurodiversity may find eye contact much more challenging than their neurotypical peers. (Neurodiversity is when students' brains process the world differently than their typically developing peers.)

Students who experience neurodiversity are likely to find eye contact more challenging.

In her *Psychology Today* article The Subtle Dance of Eye Contact in Conversation published at psychologytoday.com, Dr. Tara Well states that "Research finds that direct gaze is associated with confidence, interest, and attraction, while an averted gaze of looking away is related to lack of confidence, rejection, and being socially ostracized. In addition, many people consider eye contact to be a sign of trustworthiness" (Well, 2021, para. 2). Many adults believe that in order to be respectful, a student should maintain eye contact. In fact, avoiding eye contact is often interpreted as being overtly disrespectful or even offensive. This is a common belief, and a widely held value in white western European cultures.

However, the importance of eye contact is culturally specific. In their cross-cultural study of eye contact, researchers Shota Uono and Jari K. Hietanen (2015) found that our perception of eye contact and our bias in detecting emotion differs across Western and Eastern cultures. For example, as published on doi.org "In Japanese culture, people are taught not to maintain eye contact with others because too much eye contact is often considered disrespectful." (2015, para. 5). Connected Communicators must consider the diverse cultural values of our students and how this impacts communication.

Why We Should Not Look

In "Four Reasons Eye Contact Can Cause Overstimulation," published at thefnc.com, Dr. Jeremy Schmoe writes that, "Some people avoid eye contact simply to avoid short-circuiting their dysregulated neurology." (2022, para. 1) Dr. Schmoe tells us that this is especially true for students who experience autism, PTSD, social anxiety, or when any student is trying to concentrate on something difficult.

When the content of the conversation is a heavy lift, we generally do not ask the student to carry the additional load of eye contact. We want students to focus on the message we are trying to send with our words. Allowing them to filter out our facial expressions and look away increases their capacity to process the content of our conversation. It can be difficult to look someone directly in the eye when we are organizing our thoughts or coming up with a new idea. "This tendency may be more pronounced in people who aren't natural orators. Research shows you're able to speak more thoughtfully when looking away from a person." (Schmoe, 2022, para. 16-17) Sometimes, a student may only have the capacity to look at you or listen to you. Asking them to do both can be counterproductive and lead to an avoidable power struggle.

Sometimes, a student may only have the capacity to look at you or listen to you. Not both.

Use a Third Point

Given the complexity of eye contact, having some socially acceptable alternatives can be helpful for both the student and the Connected Communicator. To ensure the student is actually listening and not just tuning out, you can employ the use of a third point.

We borrow the term "third point" from the work of Reuven Feuerstein (1991), an Israeli psychologist who developed the concept of cognitive mediation. Cognitive mediation is a three-point interaction. For educators this would be between the educator, the student, and a focus, or third point. As Lipton and Wellman (2022) share in *Learning-Focused Supervision*, "Physically referencing the third point in a space off to the side between the parties provides a psychologically safe place for information, concerns, and problems. This careful use of space and gesture depersonalizes ideas." (p. 16)

A third point is an object, most often a piece of paper, positioned between the people communicating. This artifact could be anything—a written assignment, a drawing, an article, or any object that illustrates the purpose of the conversation. The third point shifts the energetic weight of the discussion from the people to the object. Kids are better able to discuss difficult topics when they don't feel the pressure or tension is directed at them. This strategy creates a shared experience and understanding. The third point also allows kids to view their actions as something they did, not something they are.

As an example, imagine a student has turned in an essay full of grammatical and spelling errors. In discussing the needed changes, the student will be much more receptive to hearing about their errors when they can look at the paper instead of the teacher. It naturally changes the teacher's language to focus more on the work, and less on the individual doing the work. Notice the difference here without the use of the third point: "Saul, I read your essay last night and you consistently spelled words incorrectly." With the use of the third point: "Saul, let's take a look at your essay. Do you see the spelling errors here and here?" Using the third point in this example allows the student to distance himself from the feedback. In turn, he is then more able to receive the edits as a constructive critique of his writing and not an attack on his person. For younger students, building a visual representation together of the issue at hand using a white board, scratch paper, or dolls is another example of using a third point.

Third Point

Credit: Alec Dickinson

Connecting It: To Look or Not to Look

Eye contact can be controversial. We must examine our purpose when asking students to use it. Is our purpose of the exchange for them to hear us or to see us? We believe allowing the student to focus on our words instead of our face will allow them to take in the information we are sharing, and avoid power struggles. When a student is averting their gaze, the Connected Communicator reminds themselves that there are times when students can look at us or listen to us, but not both.

Connected Takeaways

- Eye Contact is individually, situationally, and culturally specific.
- Do you want them to see you or hear you? There are times when students can either look at us *or* listen to us, but not both.
- Eye contact can be dysregulating or intimidating.
- Use a third point.

PART III

Connecting Conversations-How to Coach for Connection

"I've learned that people will forget what you said, people will forget what you did, but people will never forget how you made them feel."

-Maya Angelou

CHAPTER 10

Acknowledge, Validate, Coach

"By listening with calm and understanding, we can ease the suffering of another person."

–Thich Nhat Hanh

Can you think of a time when you felt frustrated or irritated about a situation and you just needed to vent to someone? When you were describing what happened, did the person actually listen to you, or did they offer advice and solutions to help you solve your problem? If it was the latter, how did that make you feel? We are going to guess that it only increased your level of frustration–we know it does for us. As it turns out, kids aren't all that different from grown-ups in this regard. And yet, we have all tried to problem-solve with students when all they really want is to vent or be heard.

Sometimes, we try to solve problems for students when they simply want to be heard.

Tiffany remembers a time when she was a high school teacher, talking to one of her students, who we'll call Kaylan. Kaylan was sharing her frustrations about something her soccer teammates did that she was pretty upset about. Tiffany listened to Kaylan and then offered several different solutions that Kaylan could try to resolve the issue with her teammates. Kaylan kept dismissing the suggestions and became more and more frustrated and escalated. Tiffany realized that she had skipped some steps and had gone directly to coaching. She needed to change course so she stopped trying to coach and started to acknowledge and validate instead. She began recapping the feelings Kaylan had shared, including that she was mad, frustrated, and scared about what her teammates were doing. Then, Tiffany said her feelings were totally understandable, and she could see why Kaylan felt that way. Tiffany continued to empathize with Kaylan by naming, and then affirming, the feelings that Kaylan was having. Once Kaylan felt heard and understood, her demeanor changed and she was ready to problem solve. Tiffany asked if she wanted help figuring out what to do next. Kaylan did, and they were then able to problem-solve together.

This strategy, coined by licensed psychotherapist and author, Nando Raynolds is called, "Acknowledge, Validate, Coach." (Nando Raynolds, personal communication, December 29, 2022) We find it invaluable when working with students. While this process is pretty straightforward to explain, it can be difficult to do—especially when kids are escalated.

Acknowledge

The first step is to *acknowledge*, or name the feeling that a child is experiencing. Everyone wants to be understood. Letting students know that you see what's going on for them can be huge. It is important to get this right, so if they are using specific words to describe how they are feeling, use those exact same feeling words as you reflect back what you hear them saying. In the case of Kaylan, you could say, "It sounds like you are really frustrated about this." Or "Wow. You must be really irritated by that." Or "I hear you saying that made you angry." The reflective listening techniques described in our section on *Authentic Listening* are helpful here. Of course, students do not always use words to describe how they are feeling. In that case, you are going to have to take an educated guess based on context clues. You might say something like, "I can see you are really frustrated by this." Or "It seems like you are feeling irritated and maybe a little angry right now."

If you are working with a student who does not yet have the vocabulary for their feelings, Rosenberg (2015) offers a tool in his book *Nonviolent Communication* to teach this vocabulary. You may also want to utilize a feelings or emotions chart as a visual resource to help a child narrow down their feelings. A quick internet search will result in hundreds of free downloadable resources for this. We recommend displaying one that includes pictures and labels you can use as a tool when working with students. When we have names for our feelings, it's much easier to navigate them.

> *When we have names for our feelings,*
> *it's much easier to navigate them.*

When we acknowledge how a child is feeling, by naming it or reflecting back what we heard them say, we are telling them that we recognize them. They feel heard because we are actively listening to them and reflecting back what they are experiencing.

Validate

The next step is to *validate*. After all, you can't argue with what someone else is feeling. This is the time to let the student know their feelings are valid and you understand why they are feeling that way. Big feelings can be worrisome so it is important for us to help normalize them for students. With Kaylan, you might say something like, "It's really understandable that you would feel that way." Or "I can see why you would feel frustrated and angry about what happened with your teammates." Or "It makes sense to me that you would feel angry about that." Or even, "I think it's pretty common for someone in your situation to feel super irritated."

Validating feelings validates students.

This is how we make sure students feel understood. When we validate the feelings children are having, we are validating them as people. We are helping them feel seen, heard, and valued. We are letting them know that we are taking their feelings seriously, and, in turn, taking *them* seriously.

Coach

The final step is to *coach*, or teach. This is the time to redirect the student, provide another perspective, offer support or advice, or coach them to a new understanding. This has to come *after* acknowledging and validating the student's feelings. Oftentimes, we start with the coach step first in an attempt to redirect behavior, problem-solve, or help our students feel better. However, when we skip or gloss over the first two steps (acknowledging and validating), we inadvertently ignore or invalidate their feelings. We may even be offering coaching that doesn't address the actual problem because we don't yet fully understand it. If you start to coach too soon, it can also lead to defensiveness, making the coaching ineffective.

When we begin with coaching, before acknowledging and validating, we run the risk of ignoring or invalidating feelings.

With Kaylan, that was certainly true. When Tiffany jumped to coaching before taking the time to just sit with Kaylan and her feelings, it didn't work. In fact, it made Kaylan feel even more irritated. However, once Tiffany gave Kaylan space to have and share her feelings, and then acknowledged and validated them, Kaylan was available to move on to coaching. It was only then she could begin looking for solutions. It is also helpful to check in and see if the student is ready for coaching. Tiffany did this with Kaylan by asking, "This sounds really challenging. Would it be helpful for me to brainstorm some possible next steps with you?" You could also say, "Are you interested in some feedback about ways to go about addressing this?" This gives students a choice in the next steps. Don't force it unless you have to. Sometimes they don't even need you to offer solutions or coach them. They may simply need to feel heard and affirmed.

For a much younger student who is upset because they don't want to go inside when recess ends, the conversation might sound something like:

Acknowledge	**Student**: But I don't wanna go inside! I want to swing and I didn't get a chance to swing today!
	Adult: Oh, you are upset that you didn't get to swing today.
	Student: Yes! I am!
	Adult: I can see that. It looks like you are mad and sad that you didn't get to swing before recess ended.
	Student: Yeah. Mad and sad. Both. At the same time!
Validate	**Adult**: I get it. If I really wanted to swing and then I wasn't able to and then recess ended, I would be pretty mad and sad too.
	Student: Yeah. Cuz I really wanted to swing and they all took way longer and didn't share.
Acknowledge	**Adult**: Yep. You really wanted to swing and then you didn't get to and it made you feel mad and sad.
	Student: Yeah.

Validate	**Adult:** Well, that makes sense to me.
Coach	**Adult:** I wonder if we could come up with a plan to make sure you get to swing at the next recess? **Student:** What kind of plan? **Adult:** Well, I wonder if we could meet outside and I could help make sure that kids take their turns with the swing. **Student:** Really? **Adult:** Yep. I can do that. Right now we need to get inside because our class is starting and it doesn't work for you to be out here by yourself. **Student:** OK.

Connecting It: Acknowledge, Validate, Coach

When we take time to acknowledge and validate a student's feelings, we are actually acknowledging and validating them as humans. Students who feel acknowledged and validated are open to coaching. When students and educators can problem-solve through coaching, we have strengthened our Connected Relationship for Learning.

Connected Takeaways

+ We must acknowledge feelings, then validate them, before we can coach.
+ If we skip the first two steps, kids don't feel heard and won't hear us.
+ Validating feelings validates students.
+ Sometimes when we acknowledge and validate, kids are able to solve problems without the need for coaching.

CHAPTER 11

Impulses Aren't Choices

"It's only when we are able to see our own behavior that we are able to wake up and start making conscious choices."

-Debbie Ford

We work with young humans. Oftentimes, an unexpected behavior is as much a surprise to the student as it is to the grown-up. Separating the *impulse* to do something, and the *choice* to do that thing is hard for young people. It can be hard for older people, too. It requires lots of practice and patience.

Part of our job as educators is to recognize whether the unexpected behavior was an impulse or a conscious choice. At first blush, this delineation may seem unimportant. However, as we have learned from Tim Feeney, PhD. (personal communication, March 23, 2019), this is actually a crucial distinction. When we are able to determine if a child was acting on impulse or making a conscious choice, we are better equipped to address the behavior. Knowing the difference informs our teaching and allows us to determine the best approach. Additionally, it is imperative that we correctly label the behavior for the child so they are better able to change this behavior moving forward. Think about how self-perception might change if the self-talk is, "I make bad choices" versus "I wish I hadn't acted so impulsively."

When we help students realize they acted on impulse, we help them change their future behavior.

Impulses occur in immediate response to something. When students act on impulse, they act without thinking. Take for example, a middle school student, Adele. Adele is walking down the hallway when another student speeds past her on his wheelie shoes. The other student accidentally bumps Adele's elbow and keeps rolling past without so much as a backwards glance. Adele, meanwhile, loses her grip on her armful of books, papers, colored pencils, and granola bar. Her items go flying and are now scattered all over the ground steps away from her locker. Out of frustration, Adele shouts out some rich, colorful, and not-in-any-way school-appropriate language at the kid who just sent her supplies soaring.

Mr. Gonzalez, a support professional, sees this and is surprised that Adele yelled obscenities. Mr. Gonzalez, a skilled Connected Communicator, asks Adele what is going on, and resists the urge to immediately reprimand her. Adele explains what happened, and the two of them begin picking up her belongings.

What do you think? Did Adele make a conscious choice to scream obscenities down the hallway, or did she react on impulse to the situation? We tend to think that Adele acted on impulse. This distinction matters. If Mr. Gonzalez was to treat the unexpected behavior as a conscious choice, he would say to Adele, " Wow. That was a really poor choice you made to scream those foul words at your classmate." Adele might then feel ashamed or baffled as to why she would have thought it was OK to make such a horrible choice. Of course she already knows better than to curse and name-call at school. Adele may even begin to think that she is a bad person.

Stop, Think, and Make a Good Choice

Impulses can be so hard for kids (and everyone else) to control, especially when we are feeling under pressure, confused, or angry. However, one of our jobs as Connected Communicators is to help students learn how to think before acting. One strategy that we have found quite effective in teaching this is to use the language: "Stop, Think and Make a Good Choice." We first read this catch phrase in the children's book *Stop, Think and Make Good Choices* by Melania Lavezz (2015). We took this phrase and turned it into a teaching strategy that we employ often when working with kids.

Most kids want to make good choices. When they remember to stop and think first, they are way more likely to make a good choice. There are many strategies we can use to coach students about how to stop and think first. Some examples might be counting, breathing, taking a break, going for a walk, or getting a drink of water to name a few. Consider how Mr. Gonzalez uses this, along with other Connected Principles, to support Adele in the conversation below:

Mr. Gonzalez: Wow. That certainly was unexpected. You must have been pretty upset and just reacted on impulse. I'd guess you weren't really thinking clearly when you said that.

Adele: Yeah. That's true. I was so irritated and really angry so I just yelled.

Mr. Gonzalez: That makes sense. I think if you would have stopped and thought first, you could have managed that impulse and made a different choice.

Adele: For sure. I'd still be mad, though.

Mr. Gonzalez: Absolutely. I think you'd still be irritated and really angry. But now, on top of being mad, you're having to deal with the consequences of yelling really inappropriate words down the hallway.

Adele: Yeah. I wish I hadn't done that.

Mr. Gonzalez: Totally. Let's talk about what you might be able to do in the future so that you don't have to also deal with the consequences of acting on your impulses.

Adele will likely find herself in similar situations in the future. Say she is an adult driving in traffic and someone cuts her off. Instead of letting road rage get the best of her, Adele might remember to stop, think, and make a good choice—rather than just acting on impulse. In this case, she could pause and take a breath, try counting, or even allow herself to mutter under her breath. Any of these would give her time to make a conscious choice about how to respond, instead of reacting on impulse.

When Mr. Gonzalez framed Adele's response as an impulse, and not a conscious choice, it encouraged Adele to focus on the real issue: managing her impulses when she is angry.

Conscious Choices and Impulses: What's What?

Conscious choices are actions that students think about beforehand and follow through on. Think about the last time you responded to an unexpected behavior. Was the student acting impulsively, or was it a conscious choice? Impulsive actions require a different response from us than actions that reflect a choice by the student. Some common examples of conscious choices are:

+ Making a plan to get in a fight after school
+ Making plans to ditch class

+ Vandalizing a bathroom
+ Bringing drugs or weapons to school

Alternatively, some examples of behaviors that are often impulsive are:

+ Physically acting out in response to aggression
+ Responding to an insult by name calling
+ Using obscenities when something unexpected and unpleasant occurs
+ Blurting out in class

These are not comprehensive lists, as we do not have enough pages for all unexpected behaviors.

They Acted on Impulse. Now What?

It is important to note, we are not suggesting that adults dismiss or ignore behavior just because it was impulsive, nor are we saying that students who act on impulse shouldn't have consequences. Students are still responsible for their actions, regardless of whether it was an impulse or conscious choice. We are recommending that adults help students more accurately identify their actions as what they actually are: impulses and conscious choices. To do this, we can help students see that their actions were impulsive, help them understand the impact it had on themselves or others, and then work with them to make it right.

Students are responsible for their actions, regardless of whether that action was an impulse or a conscious choice.

But It Was an Accident!

Oftentimes, students will incorrectly name their impulses as accidents. We can understand why they might feel this way. To a child, it might seem like an accident because the child didn't really mean to do the thing they did. They acted on impulse. It's important for Connected Communicators to correctly label the behavior for what it actually is: an impulse, not an accident. An accident is an incident that happens by chance. An impulse is a reaction that occurs without thinking. Helping students see the difference better enables them to take accountability for their actions so they have a better chance of making good choices in the future.

When helping children differentiate between an accident and an impulse, it can be helpful to provide an example. It might sound like this: "Well I know you might think it was an accident, but it really doesn't look like it was. I think you mean you wish you hadn't done it, but it wasn't an accident. An accident is when you spill your drink. What you are talking about is acting without thinking, and then wishing you hadn't done it."

Consider an elementary student, Henry. Henry is playing hide-and-seek at recess. James, one of Henry's classmates, jumps out from behind a tree and yells, "Boo!" at Henry. Henry gets scared and punches James. James begins to cry and so does Henry. The playground monitor comes over and asks what happened. James yells, "Henry hit me! We were just playing a game and he punched me!" Henry responded, "No! That's not true! It was an accident. He scared me and I accidentally moved my hand into him."

As Connected Communicators, we hypothesize that Henry didn't make a conscious choice to hit James. We also don't believe it was an accident. It's pretty hard to accidentally hit someone. It does appear to be an impulsive reaction. Nevertheless, Henry needs to understand that his impulse was dangerous and it is unacceptable to use physical aggression to solve problems. In order to effectively change the behavior in the future, we need to help Henry understand why he reacted the way that he did.

Once the boys were calm and James had been attended to, the playground monitor was able to ask more questions to determine what happened. The Connected Conversation might look like this:

Playground Monitor: Henry, I hear that you were scared. It must have really been surprising when James jumped out at you.

Henry: Ya! It really scared me.

Playground Monitor: Right. Sounds like you acted without thinking and hit James.

Henry: Well, no. I was scared, but I accidentally hit him.

Playground Monitor: Hmm . . . You know what? It doesn't look like that was a real accident. An accident is when you accidentally bump someone. This was different. It wasn't an accident when you hit James, but I think you *wish you hadn't done it*. I think you were scared and you reacted without thinking when you hit James.

Henry: Yeah. I guess that's right.

Playground Monitor: So that's not an accident. That means you did it, but you wish you hadn't.

Henry: For real–I really wish I hadn't done that.

Playground Monitor: I can tell. I think that is why you were crying, too. I think you felt bad. Did you mean to hurt James?

Henry: No way! He's my friend. I would never mean to hurt him.

Playground Monitor: I get that. It seems to me that you might have forgotten to think first. I think that if you would have stopped and thought first, you would have made a good choice.

Henry: Yeah. I didn't think at all. I just hit.

Playground Monitor: Hmm . . . I wonder how that might have gone differently if you would have remembered to stop and think first?

Henry: I don't think I would have hit James.

Playground Monitor: I think you're right. Even though you didn't think first and you feel bad, it is not OK to hit. We all have to learn how to stop and think. Let's head inside so we can talk more about what you can do differently next time you are scared.

Connecting It: Impulses Aren't Choices

It is important to teach kids that impulses and conscious choices are different. When we help students realize they acted on impulse, we help them change their future behavior. If we incorrectly name student impulses as conscious choices, we inadvertently reinforce negative self-perception, and increase the likelihood they will repeat similar behaviors in the future. However, when we name impulses accurately, our goal is to help students begin to recognize impulses for what they are: reactions that occur without reflection. This supports them in learning how to put space between an impulse and an action, and they are more likely to remember to think before they act. This makes them better equipped to remember to make good choices and keep their impulses in check.

Connected Takeaways

- Impulses and conscious choices are different.
- When we help students realize they acted on impulse, we help them change their future behavior.
- If we incorrectly name student impulses as conscious choices, we inadvertently reinforce the negative self-perception. "I make bad choices" versus "I wish I hadn't acted so impulsively."
- We can help students curb their impulses by encouraging them to stop, think, and make a good choice.
- Younger students often need help distinguishing between an accident and something they wish they hadn't done.

CHAPTER 12

Sitting in the Fire

"Sometimes, simply by sitting, the soul collects wisdom."

-Zen Proverb

When you need to make a change in your life, are you more likely to do so when someone tells you that you need to change, or when you come to that realization on your own? For most of us, it's more impactful when we discover for ourselves the changes we wish to make. This is only possible when we have the space and tools to reflect on our values and who it is we want to be. It is no different for the young people we serve.

When students make mistakes that require a change, they need an opportunity to reflect and experience the impact of their actions. They need to internalize that their behavior is not aligned to their values. In order to allow this growth opportunity, they need space to reflect on or sit with their actions and consider the impact it had on others. Once they have time to really think about the impact of their choices, they will behave differently moving forward.

Don't Rescue Them from the Learning

Sometimes when we have a difficult conversation with a child and they realize they made a mistake, they cry or become visibly upset. As educators (as well as caring and empathetic humans), it can be easy for us to try and save students from uncomfortable feelings. It is so hard to sit by and watch a child feel sad, ashamed, or worried. However, when well-intentioned educators jump in and rescue kids from their feelings, they can also unintentionally rescue them from the learning, too.

When we rescue students from their feelings, we risk rescuing them from the learning, too.

Next time you are with a student who made a poor choice and you see they are beginning to feel the weight of their actions, don't jump in right away and help them feel better. This can be difficult to do; for many of us, we have to restrain ourselves from saving kids from their own big feelings. However, Connected Communicators must give kids time to *Sit in the Fire*. We learned this strategy, and many others, from our dear friend and school counselor, Mary Giancarlo. (Mary Giancarlo, personal communication, December 7, 2022) She has been supporting students and their families for several decades.

Sitting in the Fire

When we give kids an opportunity to feel the impact of their actions, we allow them to *Sit in the Fire*. We want students to have the time and space to reflect on and feel the weight of their actions. When we allow students to feel this weight, it ultimately helps them realize they need to make a change. This is where the learning happens.

This healthy level of discomfort is not the same thing as letting students sit with unhealthy shame. Instead, this is strategic discomfort. It is similar to a productive struggle in teaching. In other words, allowing a student to *Sit in the Fire* is giving the student just enough information, time, and space to discover the way forward for themselves, just as a skilled teacher would do when teaching a math concept.

A Time to *Not* Talk

In practice, using *Sitting in the Fire* is most appropriate when a student shares something big or important about their own behavior. It could also be when they cry or look visibly upset in reaction to something they did. When this happens, do not fill the silence. Avoid jumping in right away and telling them what they did wrong. Don't tell them not to worry. Instead, invoke the wisdom of the Buddhist saying, "Don't just do something, stand there." Just sit in the fire with them, and hold space for them to reflect on their actions.

CTC Sentence Stems to get them reflecting:

- I can see you are having some big feelings. That's really normal and understandable. It seems like maybe you wish you might have done something differently. I wonder what that might be?
- Oh wow–that was kind of a big deal. How are you feeling about this now?
- Hmmm . . .that really hurt your classmate's feelings. Was that your intention?

Shame Spiral or Productive Struggle?

Walking the fine line between productive struggle and unhealthy shame requires that an educator really knows the student with whom they are working. The educator must balance how much fire is too much and may lead to shame. At that same time, we must also consider how much is too little and may rob the student of the opportunity to learn from the behavior. This is tricky. We must be intentional and thoughtful when applying this technique. It requires us to pay close attention to a child's verbal and nonverbal cues while they are Sitting in the Fire.

In our experience, we have seen a few warning signs that the student is entering a shameful place. One is that the child starts to shut down completely. This might look like a head down, or a sudden change in their willingness to talk with you. Another significant warning sign is if the child begins to engage in negative self-talk. They might say they are a terrible person, or they are bad, or in an extreme case even say they don't deserve to be here (if ever a student talks about self-harm, you will want to immediately pause and refer to your organization's suicide risk assessment protocols). These are all warnings that they are mistaking their behavior for *who* they are instead of *what* they did. Both of these reactions require that you immediately intervene.

If the student begins to go to an unhealthy or shameful place, step in using COLBA (Care Out Loud Behavioral Approach), telling them they are a good kid and even really good kids make mistakes. This could also be a good opportunity to validate them and let them know you understand why they might have done what they did, and then coach them toward a different way of handling the problem in the future. The key message is that they are a good person, you care about them, and what they did is not aligned to who they want to be.

But I Didn't Mean It: Intention vs. Impact

Sometimes when working with students to *Sit in the Fire*, they will say, "That's not what I meant when I did that," or "I didn't mean it that way," or "But that wasn't my intention." Sometimes the impact of our actions on others is quite different than what our intention may have been. We might be very well-intentioned; however, the impact of our words or actions was harmful.

Our job as Connected Communicators is to help students take another's perspective in order to understand that regardless of our intention, our impact is what is lasting and ultimately what matters to others. It simply does not matter if we had the best intentions when we caused harm. We must then work to make it right. Connected Communicators help students take perspective through listening, reflecting, and recognizing how their actions impacted others. We can still acknowledge and validate their intention and then coach them to examine the impact on others.

Regardless of our intention, our impact is what is lasting and ultimately what matters.

CTC Sentence Stems to help students examine the impact of their actions:

- I understand it wasn't your intention; however, the impact of your actions caused . . .
- I get that's not what you meant, but it made them feel . . .
- I know you didn't mean to, but their feelings are really hurt.

Intention and impact is a topic that is widely explored by leaders in the field of anti-racism. We recommend all Connected Communicators study anti-racism further and read works on this topic. Dr. Ibram Kendi, Jason Reynolds, Zaretta Hammond, Ijeoma Oluo, Ta-Nehisi Coates, and Matthew Reynolds are all experts in this field. These powerful authors and leaders have significantly shaped our world view and the way in which we build a culture of connection.

Connecting It: Sitting in the Fire

Students need opportunities to reflect on their actions so they can come to recognize their mistakes. They need time and space to realize that their words or actions are impacting others and not serving them. It is easier to give a student the correct answer in math than it is to let them engage in a productive struggle to solve the problem themselves. In the same way, it is easier to save students from their uncomfortable feelings, than allowing them to feel the discomfort and come to their own realizations. Connected Communicators know that when we take this easier route, we are robbing students of the opportunity to truly learn. Growth is hard, and it is our job to facilitate it. Sometimes that means letting students *Sit in the Fire*.

Connected Takeaways

+ Kids need to reflect on their actions and their impact.
+ Don't rescue students from the learning by rescuing them from their big feelings.
+ Let students *Sit in the Fire*.
+ Monitor students' verbal and nonverbal cues to know if they are entering a shameful place and intervene when necessary.

PART IV

Connecting During the Scary Bits–Connected Communication When the Heat is On

"When the going gets tough, the tough get going."
-American English Proverb

CHAPTER 13

The Student Playbook-
Common Moves

*"I love talking with kids; Adults never ask
me what my third favorite color is."*

-Aryan Songara

D o you ever feel like your students have a secret playbook of moves to use when faced with their unexpected behavior? In the thousands of conversations we've had with kids, the patterns that emerge have led us to believe that there is one out there. It may not be written down, but there are certain moves that you are guaranteed to encounter in your quest to build connected relationships with kids. The great news is, when we know the move in advance, we can be prepared with a few moves of our own. Let's examine some of the most common student moves we have encountered, along with some supportive moves the educator can use to keep things on track.

Claim Amnesia

"I forgot." "I don't remember." "I don't think I remember that." It's amazing how poor a student's recall can suddenly become when faced with a question they don't want to answer, or something that is difficult. In these situations, it is not uncommon for the student to indicate that they don't remember. Saying "I forgot" is different from "It didn't happen." To us, this is an indication that they know they made an error, but they are not ready to come out and say it. It could also be a clue that they are wondering how much you know about the situation—a young person's version of trying not to tip their hand.

> ## *"I forgot" is very different from "That didn't happen."*

We have found the best supportive move in response to claiming amnesia is to use a combination of open-ended questions and wait time. You can also make it clear you know what happened (even if you don't have the details) and give them a reminder so they have an out to tell you more.

Let's imagine you have been asked to debrief with a middle school student about some harsh words she used during homeroom, and her move is to claim amnesia:

Teacher: Tell me about what happened with Justine in homeroom today.
Tania: I don't remember.
Teacher: You don't remember being in homeroom today?
Tania: Nope, I have a bad memory.
Teacher: That must be hard. Now I know you are a kind person. Every once in awhile, even someone who is a kind person

messes up. The most important thing to do when that happens is to take responsibility. I want to give you a minute to think more. If it helps you remember, I'm hearing that several folks heard you say something pretty unkind. Does that help you remember? (Teacher provides lots of wait time.)

Tania: I'm not sure.

Teacher: OK. Sounds like you are having a hard time remembering. I want you to think it over, and we can talk about this again during lunch today.

Tania: Oh wait! I totally forgot. When I was at lunch, Justine was being so annoying talking about the sleepover she went to last weekend. I finally just told her that she's a . . . I used the B word. I'm so sorry, I was just so mad. She thinks she is so cool because she got invited and I didn't.

Teacher: I'm so glad you told me. I can imagine you were feeling left out. That is really hard, and I'm so sorry that happened. (Pause) Even though that is really hard, that does not make it OK to call other students bad names. How are we going to make this right with Justine?

There are a few things to notice about this exchange. First, the teacher did not call the student on the fact that she clearly did remember. We know it can be tempting to say something like, "It's a miracle-your amnesia is cured!" We get it, but it's the opposite of helpful. If you focus on the fact they said they forgot, instead of talking about the topic at hand, you are arguing about the state of a student's memory. Notice also that the teacher provides a prompt that is just enough, and a pathway to telling the truth. As in every exchange about unexpected behavior, the teacher was also careful to separate the student from the behavior.

Denial

What if the student straight up denies everything? This is probably one of the most common moves we see, and we get the instinct. No one wants to feel like they are in trouble. There are three steps that we like to take to help a student share the whole truth:

- *Help Me Help You*: Remind them that you are on their side. Always. Let them know that you really want to help them figure this out, but you can't help them if they are not being honest with you.

- *Lay Out the Evidence*: If you know this student did the thing, lay out all of the reasons you know this. If it was reported by another educator, ask why they would lie about something like this. It is a good idea to start with something like, "I'm confused, because I was told or I saw this behavior and you are telling me something different. Help me understand."

- *Take Your Time*: This is a good time to allow students to think it through. Saying something like, "It is clear you need some time to consider how to best tell me what is going on. I'm going to leave you here to think about what you want to tell me. While you are thinking, remember that we all make mistakes, and the only way forward is to be honest and take responsibility." This is also a good time to indicate that in some way you are going to gather some additional evidence. For example, "I'm going to go check with Ms. Julie, because what you are telling me and what she told me are different."

- *Give an Out:* Students are now struggling with the fact that they told you a lie on top of whatever the behavior is. Saying something like, "I can understand why you might have been nervous about being honest with me. It takes a lot of courage to admit when you have made a mistake. When we talk to your parents about this, I want to be able to say that you took responsibility. I am giving you another opportunity to be completely honest."

- *Lay Out the Consequences:* When a student is not being honest, lay out the consequences for the original infraction, as well as additional consequences for dishonesty. . Explain that their lack of integrity and any time spent on additional investigation will be considered when determining next steps. You might say, "Well, it seems like I have more investigating to do. I am going to talk to all the other witnesses involved. This will take me a lot of time, and that's OK *if* you are telling the truth. It's really important for you to know if the results of my investigation indicate that you are not being honest with me, there will be additional consequences. Before I do that, I want to give you another opportunity to tell the whole truth now."

Let's consider a scenario where a student, T.J., got frustrated on the playground and hit another student. They have been escorted to the office by the educational assistant who saw the situation unfold.

Help Me Help You	Connected Communicator: Tell me a little bit about what happened? T.J.: Nothing, I didn't do anything. Connected Communicator: T.J., this must be scary. It is really overwhelming and hard when we know we have made a big mistake. I want to help you figure this out. I can only do that if we are honest with each other. T.J.: Whatever, I didn't do anything.
Lay Out the Evidence	Connected Communicator: I'm so confused. I just talked to Ms. Jenkins, and she told me that she saw you hit Sam. She also saw that you two were arguing right before he got hurt. There are several other students who saw what happened. Can you help me understand why these folks are telling me something different? T.J.: I don't know.
Take Your Time	Connected Communicator: I think you need some time to consider how to best tell me what is going on. I know it is really hard. I'm going to check on Sam. Stay here and think about what you want to tell me.

COLBA	While you are thinking, remember that I know you are a really good kid and even really good kids make mistakes. We all make mistakes, and the only way forward is to be honest and take responsibility. Connected Communicator leaves T.J. on his own for a while.
Give an Out	Connected Communicator: OK, T.J., I can understand why you might be nervous about being honest with me. It takes a lot of courage to admit when you have made a mistake. When we talk to your parents about this, I want to be able to say that you took responsibility and that you were honest. This is a free chance to start over, and tell me what is going on. T.J.: Fine! Sam was being so mean, and when he called me a jerk, I hit him and he fell. Connected Communicator: I'm so glad you told me, I know that is really hard. Let's figure out together what we can do to make it right.

In this exchange, you will notice that the Connected Communicator did a couple of things to help T.J. tell the truth. They made it clear that they did know what happened. They also used COLBA and showed a lot of understanding about how hard it is to tell the truth when you have made a mistake. When the student did finally tell the truth, the Connected Communicator focused on how glad they are that the student told them, not the fact that they lied. Again, stay focused on the issue at hand. Make it clear that you know the student is not telling the truth, but do not call them a liar, or accuse them outright of lying. If backed into a corner, they are likely to double down on their story to avoid getting in trouble for lying, or to continue to distract from the issue at hand.

Crocodile Tears

We know we can't reason with a student when they are escalated, and yet sometimes it feels like the escalation is manufactured as an avoidance tactic. If a student responds to your attempts at a connected conversation with excessive tears, the best strategy is to remove the audience and wait it out.

Most grown-ups can distinguish between a true expression of emotion from kids, and tears that are less genuine. We are not saying you should ignore the tears, or not show empathy. Check in with the student, acknowledge and validate their feelings, and support them in getting to a place for discussion. If you get stuck in a loop, when as soon as the conversation shifts to the topic at hand, the tears come back on, then it is time to step away. Again, be clear. "Misty, I can see you are still really upset about this. I want to help you, and I can only do that if we talk about it. I'm going to give you a minute, and then we are going to talk about [insert actual topic at hand]." Again, rinse and repeat until the student talks to you calmly.

Fleeing

What if the student just takes off? Students desperate to avoid facing up to what is going on may just run. This looks different at different ages. Erika will never forget when she had a student in her office at the high school that had been discovered with a bag of marijuana in his backpack. As she picked up the phone to call his parents, he suddenly grabbed the bag of marijuana off her desk and ran out of the office at top speed, leaving a trail of green leaves behind him. Valuable lesson learned! In all further meetings with this student, and others in similar circumstances, Erika positioned herself or someone from the leadership team between the student and the door. If they started to glance towards the door, or give any indication that they were considering running away, she would remind them that facing up to this difficult situation now is the only way through it. Postponing consequences will only make it harder.

Younger students are even more likely to give in to the impulse to run, especially if they are already in transit for the conversation. If the student has a history of elopement, (the technical term for running away) use strategic positioning whenever possible. Position the student away from the exit, and sit close enough to put a calming hand on their shoulder if they look like they are going to run. If they turn their body, or start to move, get yourself between the student and the door. Again, offer the same message: "I understand why you might want to run away from this situation. It's hard. We'll get through it together." Be sure that you are familiar with your organization's policies for responding when students leave campus.

Refusing to Take Accountability

What if a student has admitted what happened, but will not take accountability with the person impacted? Specifically, the student will not apologize for their actions. We don't believe in forcing an apology if the student is not sorry, but we do think we should do everything we can to pave the way for the student to take appropriate accountability.

Once you have made it clear to the student that they are a good person, and you are going to care about them no matter what, it might help to dig into where the behavior came from. Oftentimes, even most of the time, students do not anticipate the impact their actions are going to have. Let the student know that you understand the difference between intention and impact. Explaining to them that you think they did not intend to hurt anyone can help alleviate the burden of apology. Saying to the student, "I know that if you had any idea X would happen, you would not have done it. At the same time, X did happen so I want to support you in making it right."

As we discuss in our chapter *Impulses Aren't Choices*, pointing out to a student that they acted on impulse instead of making a thoughtful choice can help. Saying, "I know if you had stopped and thought for even a quick second, you never would have done that." This again reinforces the idea that even though the student did an unexpected thing, they are still a good kid.

Finally, if the student is still not able to see the impact their actions had on others enough to apologize, it may be time to engage in some perspective taking activities. With younger students, draw a quick stick figure sketch that has all the people involved in the incident when it happened, including bystanders. Put speech and thought bubbles above each person and ask them to imagine what others were thinking or feeling when this was happening. For older students, the picture is not needed, but the idea is the same. Ask them to imagine what the bystanders were thinking and feeling, what the teacher might have been thinking and feeling, and of course, what any other person directly involved might have been thinking or feeling. Helping students to recognize the impact of their actions on others builds empathy, and makes it more likely that they will be able to deliver a genuine apology. When students genuinely feel empathy and genuinely apologize, it repairs relationships and strengthens the culture of connection in school.

When students recognize the impact of their actions, it builds empathy and a culture of connection.

Connecting It: The Student Playbook-Common Moves

Great news! Now that we have a better understanding of the students' playbook, we can respond with some connected moves of our own. We have all seen these student moves countless times throughout our careers. By having some go-to responses, we are now no longer caught off-guard and are able to focus on creating a culture of connection.

Connected Takeaways

+ *Claim Amnesia:* When students claim amnesia, share the facts, and give them space to "remember." Often, it is a cue the thing really did happen and they are not ready to talk about it yet.
+ *Denial:* When students deny something they clearly did, use the following steps; help me help you, lay out the evidence, take your time, give an out.
+ *Crocodile Tears:* Once you have used authentic listening techniques and cared out loud, if they continue with excessive tears or anger, give them space, and wait it out.
+ *Fleeing:* Look for signals that the student might run. Use body position to limit their escape route. Remind them that owning up is the only way to resolve it.
+ *Refusing to Apologize:* When a student refuses to apologize, use strategies to reduce shame by separating the behavior from the person. Practice empathy and perspective taking.

CHAPTER 14

Who's the Boss?

"Yelling silences your message. Speak quietly so children can hear your words instead of just your voice."

–L.R. Knost

It has happened to all of us. We make a quick redirection in class, and a student responds with an invitation to rumble. In this moment you have a choice. You can engage with the student and see who comes out the victor, or you can demonstrate to the class and the student that you don't engage in power struggles. We hope we have the wisdom to decline the invitation, as we know that as soon as we engage, we have lost. We often think of these sorts of mini confrontations as students inviting us into a game tug of war. In our experience, "picking up the rope" is almost always a mistake.

As soon as we engage in a power struggle, we have lost.

Prevention

There are many reasons to avoid power struggles. When we stay levelheaded and leave the rope on the ground, we take the quickest route to de-escalation for the student. When the educator remains in control and prevents students from feeding off the attention of others, we break the cycle of escalation. By refusing to engage, we establish for the student (and ourselves) that we simply aren't willing to participate in a power struggle.

Of course, avoiding power struggles is easier said than done. How we make requests and frame expectations can reduce a student's likelihood of attempting to begin a mini-battle. One easy trap is to frame a non-negotiable as a question. Our advice–don't ask a question if it isn't a choice.

Don't ask a question if it is not a choice.

Instead, start your direction with *"You Can," "You May,"* or *"You need."* For example, if you want students to sit at their desks, it is far better to say "You can all take your seats now" versus "Can you please take a seat?" The answer to that question could easily be, "No!" You might elevate from "you can" to "you need" in a more immediate situation. For example, let's say you have a student climbing a fence and it is dangerous. This is not the time for a request. Instead of, "Can you please come down from there?" try, "You need to come down off the fence."

Stay Calm

When despite your best attempts, you find a student has picked up that rope and is hoping for a tug of war, there are a few tips to help you keep it on the ground. First, and perhaps most importantly, remember that we want students to catch our calm. Avoid matching the emotional level of the student and remain in control of our own emotions and responses. We suggest using some simple stress-reduction techniques before responding to a student who is attempting to engage you. Take a deep breath, get a drink of water, or take a quick break. By taking a moment to calm yourself, you have the added benefit of giving yourself a moment to make a plan.

Once you have collected yourself, use a voice that demonstrates how you would like to be feeling. By using a neutral, calm voice, you increase the likelihood of them catching your calm, and as an added benefit, by acting calm you are more likely to be calm. (published on *Intervention Central* htttps://www.interventioncentral.org). If you or the student need additional time to regulate, saying something like, "This is important, and I want to discuss it with you. We are going to have to wait until we are both feeling calmer. Let's circle back to this toward the end of class." For younger students, you might say, "We can talk when your voice sounds like mine." The added benefit of that particular statement is it forces you to make sure that your voice actually sounds calm-that would be a weird thing to yell at a student!

Say it and Run!

All right, so you are calm and in control of the situation. We then like to start with this tried-and-true avoidance technique: say it and run! In other words, share the expectation with the student, and then walk away. Move on to another student, leave the space, or turn to some very interesting papers on your desk. This makes it hard for the student to get in a zinger, or argue the expectation.

If the expectation includes two choices you can live with, then all the better. Let's take a look at an example. After reminding students that phones are to be out of sight during independent work time, a student makes a show of pulling theirs out and putting it front and center on their desk. They are clearly looking for some tug of war. The Connected Communicator would walk up quietly, kneel by the desk and say, "I am going to enter attendance. You can either put your phone in your pocket or your backpack" and then get out of there before the student can respond. In this scenario, chances are good they will tuck that phone away.

Depending on the age and what you know about the student, you might add the consequence and timeline to that statement. In the same phone scenario above, let's look at how you might say this when including consequences.

Expectation	"Our classroom agreement is that phones are put away during independent work time."
Choice	"You can either put it in your pocket or backpack"
Timeline	"before I am finished entering attendance."
Consequence	"As you know, the class agreement is that if I can still see the phone after a reminder, the phone stays with me for the rest of the day."
Walk Away	Before giving the student an opportunity to respond, walk away from the student and start taking attendance.

Using Redirection

If the student is already dug in, redirection may be the best tactic. When a behavior is low-level defiant or non-compliant, the educator may want to start by diverting the student's attention to another topic. Perhaps a high-interest activity or conversation starter is in order. You may need to pull out your classroom de-escalation tools by inviting the student to take a cool down break. At the elementary level this may be a quiet corner in the classroom with some sensory tools. At the secondary level this may be an invitation for the student to take a five-minute walk around campus.

Another helpful strategy is to let the student know that you *wish* they could get or do what they wanted. For example, if a high school student is arguing about why they should not have to be at school on time, you might say, "I wish school started later, too. I would love to be able to sleep in. Unfortunately, we start at 8:30 so we have to be here by then. Maybe you could consider writing a letter to the school board?" For a younger student, it might sound more like this. "I sure wish you could run in the halls; you are so fast! That is just not safe at school so we are going to walk." By using the phrase "I wish," you are demonstrating empathy for the student by commiserating with them. This allows you to maintain connection even while holding firm to the boundary you've set.

Time to Talk About It

There are times when we need to engage the student in productive conversation instead of either you or the student walking away. These conversations should not happen with an audience. In removing the conversation from the rest of the class, we allow students to save face, and avoid shaming or embarrassing them. You may be able to press pause by saying something like, *This is an important discussion. Let's connect on a solution that will work for both of us after class.*" When you have the opportunity to talk with the student to develop a solution, consider using the framework of Acknowledge, Validate, Coach. You have given yourself the gift of time- prepare for your conversation by completing the 4 "Ws" Planning Guide found in the appendix.

Return to Acknowledge, Validate, Coach

You have removed the audience, and planned your conversation using the 4 "Ws" Planning Guide. Now you are ready to discuss. As with most Connected Conversations, begin with listening. Acknowledge what the student is upset about. Ask open-ended questions to give the student an opportunity to share their concern, and ensure you fully understand the cause of their upset. Validate their feelings, and share that you understand the source of the conflict. It can be helpful to respond with some diffusers that indicate you heard them, even if you don't agree. Our favorites include: *"I hear you,"* *"Interesting Point,"* *or "Noted."* After the student's concerns and feelings have been acknowledged and validated, you can transition into coaching. Problem solve the situation as much as possible, and clearly state the expectation moving forward.

Compassionate Communication

We must remember that there are at least two people with feelings in every communication. When avoiding power struggles, we have found that sharing our own feelings and needs can be extremely helpful. We first learned this from Marshall Rosenberg, PhD. He developed the principles of Nonviolent Communication, or Compassionate Communication, in his large body of work dating back to the 1960s with his establishment of *The Center for Nonviolent Communication*. Dr. Rosenberg provides a thorough explanation of the principles and techniques in his book *Nonviolent Communication* (2015).

When effectively using Compassionate Communication, the speaker is focused on their own experience as opposed to analyzing someone else's. Speakers put words to their feelings and needs, leading to a request of the listener. This is in contrast to moralizing and judging someone else's actions and then making demands on the listener—a surefire recipe for a power struggle. The table below highlights the key differences.

Power Struggle Territory	Compassionate Communication
You are always blurting out in class! You need to learn to keep your mouth shut.	I feel frustrated when you are talking while I am giving directions. I need to make sure everyone hears what they are supposed to do next.
Your desk is a mess! You are so disrespectful with the classroom materials. Get this cleaned up immediately!	I have noticed that the classroom supplies have not been put away several times this week. I feel anxious when the classroom supplies are not put away. I need to ensure that our classroom materials are available for everyone to use.
I have told you a million times to stop tapping your pencil! You are driving me bananas. Stop it.	I have noticed that you have been tapping your pencil during instruction, and it's loud. I feel worried, as it is making it hard for other students to hear what is being said. I need to make sure everyone is able to focus during class.

When using Compassionate Communication, we have found the first three steps identified by Marshall Rosenberg the most effective to use with students at school. Compassionate Communication begins with the speaker making an observation, expressing a feeling related to that observation, and then stating a need. Dr. Rosenberg describes a final step that includes making a request. For educators at school, this strategy can be difficult and a bit tricky to employ. Therefore, we recommend that educators utilize coaching instead of making a request. Here is an example:

A student, Felix, is running down the hallway. When asked to go back and walk, he said no.

Observation	I noticed you ran down the hall to get back to class after lunch.
Feeling	I feel nervous.
Need	I need to keep the classroom safe for all students.

You will notice that the observation is a concrete statement of an action or fact. It is important we keep the observation free of any judgment or evaluation. If the teacher had something like, "Felix, you are always running and ignoring our rules and disrespecting the other students" then Felix is far less likely to commit to changing his behavior. The feeling statement, "I feel nervous," reflects what the teacher feels and is not what they think about whatever occurred. You can't argue with what someone else says they are feeling. When doing this well, it helps to eliminate the opportunity to argue about the why of the request, and reduces the chance of a power struggle. It also does not indicate what they believe others know, think, or feel. If the teacher had said, "I feel that you have been told this many times before," or "I feel like you should have known better," they are not expressing a feeling. Instead, this is expressing a judgment about the other person's actions. This is likely to sabotage the hoped-for outcome.

Of course, this does not always work the first time. How would you respond to a refusal? We like Rosenburg's (2015) four-part process:

Step One: Describe the situation.

Step Two: Guess the other person's feeling.

Step Three: Guess the reason for the feeling, together with the unmet need; then let the person verify whether you have correctly understood.

Step Four: Clarify the unmet need.

So, how does this apply if the student responds that they will not be practicing walking down the hall? We recommend something like this:

Describe the situation	**Teacher:** I shared several ideas about how we could work together to help you walk when inside the school and you said that you were not willing to try them. There is about one minute until class starts, and I am still nervous because I need to keep everyone safe.
Guess the other person's feeling	**Teacher:** Are you upset about what you might be missing while practicing? **Student:** Yes, I already know how to walk; I just forgot. I don't want to miss my break just to practice something I already know!

Guess the reason for the feeling, together with the unmet need, then let the other person verify that you have correctly understood	**Teacher:** I think it is important for you to be able to spend time with friends, and so it is frustrating for you to think about missing a break. Do I have that right? **Student:** Yes, that's right. I never get to hang out with them.
Clarify the unmet need	**Teacher:** I see that break time is important to you, and you don't want to spend time practicing something you already know. I want to make sure you can show me how you walk so everyone stays safe at school. I also want to make sure you don't miss the directions to our next activity. Let's practice right now and get it out of the way. Then you will be done and we won't have to worry about you missing another break in the future. You will be back in two shakes and we can get started with class. **Student:** OK

You will notice that the teacher listened with empathy. This avoided a power struggle, and helped bring the student to "Yes." There are times it is still not that easy. Let's imagine the student says no again. A Connected Communicator might sound like this:

Student: No, I'm not going now or at break.

Teacher(takes a breath)**:** Are you feeling frustrated? You want to get to class?

Student: Yes! I just want to get to class.

Teacher: I see. I'm still feeling nervous. It's my job to make sure everyone stays safe at school. You can hang out in the quiet corner for five minutes and think about an idea that you think might work for both of us.

Student: OK.

Every Moment is a Teaching Moment

Re-framing a power struggle into a teaching moment can also provide a graceful way out. So, what are we teaching them? First, we are modeling for our students that when there is a disagreement, we respond in a dignified manner. Second, we are holding students to a standard that requires that they discuss their concerns in a calm and respectful way. We love the strategy of actually turning the disagreement into practicing both a behavioral skill and an academic skill such as writing. If a student really wants to make a case about something, why not tell them to write it down using their best persuasive writing techniques? Now you have dodged the power struggle and engaged the student in a productive learning task.

Connecting It: Who's the Boss?

All educators have found themselves presented with the opportunity for a power struggle. The hardest and simultaneously easiest part is to avoid picking up the rope entirely. To help you do this, we have included the CTC Sentence Stems described in this chapter in the appendix, and as a printable tool on our website: connectingthroughconversation. com.

Connected Takeaways

+ Be on the lookout for power struggles. If you engaged, you have already lost!
+ Make sure you are in a head space to allow the student to catch your calm.
+ State the expectation and run!
+ Use redirection.
+ Connect with the student by using the phrase "I wish."
+ Remove the audience.
+ Allow the student room to save face.
+ Remember every moment is a teaching moment!

CHAPTER 15

Another Stinking Learning Opportunity (ASLO)

"Apologies aren't meant to change the past.
They are meant to change the future."

-Kevin Hancock

As educators, we know that what we say and how we say it when talking to students is critically important. And yet, we are going to get it wrong. A lot. Sometimes we are going to share the wrong information, or mess up a conversation. We like to refer to these inevitable errors as "Another Stinking Learning Opportunity," or *ASLO*. The great news is we will all have these learning opportunities.

Taking Responsibility

Communication is a process, and we can almost always go back and make it right when we misstep. When we take accountability, we are modeling this for students. This means that when we make a mistake, taking responsibility is critical.

"If a teacher is able to admit when he or she has made a mistake or failed to follow through on a commitment, apologize, and take responsibility for righting the situation, then that teacher is certain to have laid the groundwork for a trusting relationship." (Romero et al, p. 84, 2018)

Perhaps you spoke harshly, failed to listen fully, didn't follow through on a commitment, or simply made the wrong call. In any case, we must do our best to make it right. This requires us to first be reflective and realize that a mistake was made. Admitting to ourselves that we messed up is hard. Admitting to others that we messed up can be even harder. Knowing the importance of trust in building Connected Relationships for Learning, we must take responsibility in order to make a repair. We honor and affirm students' dignity and worth when we are honest and level with them after we have made a mistake.

We earn students' respect when we admit we made a mistake and apologize.

No educator is perfect. We will all make mistakes. When this happens, it is critical that we take accountability and apologize in order to maintain a trusting relationship. This is important for all students, but especially those who have experienced Adverse Childhood Experiences (ACEs). "ACEs students will look to see if teachers' actions match their words. ACEs students will often scrupulously evaluate whether the teacher maintains consistency, fairness, and integrity in the classroom." (Romero et al., 2018, p. 84)

Beyond maintaining trust, taking accountability is an important opportunity for modeling. We are continually teaching students how to take accountability when they mess up. By humanizing ourselves, modeling a proper apology, and demonstrating that our relationship with them is important enough for us to apologize, we are taking a mistake and turning it into a true opportunity. Even if it is a stinky one.

Modeling a Proper Apology

This only works if we do it right. What does taking accountability look like? There are a number of formulas for a proper apology, all of which have a few critical elements.

- *Acknowledge that a mistake was made:* Make it clear what you are apologizing for. Name the action and when it happened.
- *Express regret that it happened:* This is the literal apology. Most of the time this means saying "I'm sorry" or "I apologize."
- *Vow not to be a repeat offender:* If you apologize and then turn around and do it again, it will seem as though you weren't genuinely sorry. Only apologize if you intend to change the behavior, otherwise it will further erode trust. If, despite your best intentions, you find yourself repeating the behavior, you will need to do some deeper reflection to understand why so you can change moving forward.
- *Guess at how it made them feel:* Take a guess and what kind of impact your actions may have had on the student. Saying something like, "I imagine you might have felt... when I ..." should do the trick.
- *Check in to see if you got it right:* By letting them know you understand what they are feeling, you are demonstrating their feelings are valid and important.
- *Make it right:* Ask the student if there is anything you can do to repair the situation or rebuild trust. Then do that thing.

Let's imagine a scenario where a teacher loses their patience with their class and raises their voice more than they should have. Using the guidelines above, a proper apology would look something like this:

Acknowledge the mistake	"I spoke louder than I should have when I was trying to transition us to Social Studies yesterday. It may even have sounded like yelling."
Express regret (apologize!)	"I am so sorry. I should not use a tone I would not allow others to use in this class."
Vow not to repeat the mistake	"I will not speak that way to the class again. When I am needing everyone's attention, I will use our classroom attention signal."
Guess at how it made them feel	"I am thinking my tone of voice may have made some of you feel angry, scared, or confused."
Check in on how the student is feeling	"Does that resonate with you, or did any of you feel something different?"
Make it right	"Is there anything I can do to help make it right?"

What if the ASLO was made in a private exchange? In this scenario, a school counselor was dismissive of a student's indication that they were considering going to trade school instead of a four-year school. They realized this upon reflection and sought the student out to make a repair. That apology might look like this:

Acknowledge the mistake	"Yesterday, when we were talking about your plans, I think I may have been disrespectful in how I responded to your answer about your plans post-high school."
Express regret (apologize!)	"I am so sorry. I think going to a trade school is an excellent career path. Unfortunately, I don't think I communicated that well when we were talking."
Vow not to repeat the mistake	"I will be more intentional in showing my support in the future."
Guess at how it made them feel	"I am thinking I might have made you feel as though your plan to attend a trade school is not a good one, or that it is not as respectable as going to a four-year school. I don't think that."
Check in on how the student is feeling	"Does that resonate with you, or did you feel something different?"
Make it right	"You shared with me that you are excited to be an electrician. It is a very respectable and important vocation, and I hope you are proud of your decision. You are smart and capable of doing whatever you want to do. Is there anything I can do to help make this right?"

You will notice that none of these apologies included an excuse for the behavior. The teacher did not say, "I am sorry I yelled when we were moving to Social Studies, but you all were being so loud and not listening to me." It is helpful to remember that as soon as you add a "but" to the sentence, everything before it is negated. If the student behavior also needs to change, after fully apologizing, the teacher could review classroom agreements, hold a circle, or ask the students for their ideas so that everyone's needs are being met.

> ## *When you add a "but" to an apology,*
> ## *it is like you did not apologize at all.*

Identify the Audience

It is important to apologize to the audience who got to see our ASLO. If the ASLO is made publicly, well then, we need to own our ASLO publicly. So, if it was something that impacted a whole class, or whole school, then that is who needs to hear the apology. If it was one student, then only that student needs the apology. If it harmed one student, but there was an audience it gets a bit trickier. Whenever possible we want that apology to be owned publicly. First, however, the apology needs to happen directly to the student who experienced the harm. As part of that apology, the educator can ask the student permission to apologize in front of the whole class.

Connecting It: ASLO

Apologizing is hard work, and frankly no fun. On the other hand, it is powerful modeling for our students, and critical in maintaining the trust required for strong relationships. Knowing we are going to mess up, we have to ensure that our missteps don't cause long-term harm to our Connected Relationships for Learning. The only way to do this when the mistake is ours is to apologize and mean it. Humans make mistakes. Congratulations on being human.

Connected Takeaways

+ An ASLO is: **A**nother **S**tinking **L**earning **O**pportunity.
+ Take mistakes and turn them into learning experiences for us and for our students.
+ Apologizing when we mess up is critical in maintaining trust with students.
+ Modeling an effective apology is an important way to teach students accountability.
+ Effective apologies:
  ◊ Acknowledge that a mistake was made
  ◊ Express regret that it happened
  ◊ Vow not to be a repeat offender
  ◊ Guess at how it made them feel
  ◊ Check in to see if you got the feeling right
  ◊ Offer to make it right
  ◊ Apologize to the same person or group that was impacted by your mistake.
  ◊ We will make mistakes. We are human.

CHAPTER 16

Closing the Loop

"Great communication begins with connection. Communication is like a dance. One person takes a step forward, the other takes one back. Even one misstep can land both on the floor in a tangle of confusion."

-Oprah Winfrey

Navigating unexpected behaviors with the student is often just the beginning. Connected Communicators close the loop by making sure all members of the student's team are in the know. What we share and how we share it can make or break the culture of connection in our community. There is so much to closing the loop, we need a road map to navigate it all.

How Support Professionals Close the Loop

Educational Assistants, bus drivers, cafeteria staff, and other support professionals are often the first to respond to a student's unexpected behavior. As we discuss in the chapter *Planning a Connected Conversation*, the person closest to the behavior is often the most effective person to address it. Most of the time, support professionals are able to resolve an issue in the moment. Of course, sometimes the student's behavior is such that they need to share that information with other adults on the student's team. When we close this loop, we are able to circle the student with support. There are two types of communication that may be needed: FYI (For Your Information) and action required.

FYI

We use FYI communication when we have already addressed the behavior. If the teacher is not aware of what occurred, a support professional will want to close that loop. It could be that the student is having an off day, or it could be a pattern of behavior that we need to monitor. The teacher will appreciate knowing what took place, how it was addressed, and how the student responded. When the unexpected behavior requires more than an FYI, we move to an action-required response.

Action-Required Response

When a student's behavior is beyond something a support professional should handle on their own, they use action-required communication and loop in one of the student's teachers or a building administrator. They will want to know everything you know about the situation. Be prepared to share what happened, who was involved, how the student responded, who witnessed the behavior, and any other relevant information that will help the teacher or administrator address the situation with the student. We recommend the behavior is communicated to the classroom teacher when:

- It involves a conflict between peers that may be ongoing.
- It is a behavior the student is working on with a teacher.
- The consequence impacts that student's schedule in some way.

We recommend the behavior is communicated to the administrator when:

* The behavior was dangerous.
* The behavior was hateful (i.e., hate speech, harassment, bullying).
* The behavior requires the involvement of building administration.

How you share this information depends on the system in place at your school. Some schools use a referral or behavior log. Others rely on an email or a quick conversation. Make sure you're using your school's system of communication and documentation.

How Teachers Close the Loop with Grown-Ups

When unexpected behaviors happen in the classroom, they are most often handled right there in the classroom. Yet, in the same way that it is important to pass on information to the teacher when a behavior happens *outside* the classroom, it is equally important to consider who needs to be looped in when a behavior takes place *inside* the classroom.

When considering who to tell, think about who needs to know. Who are the other educators on a student's team? Do they work with an interventionist? Do they have a special education or 504 case manager? Are they meeting with the school counselor? Would it be helpful to let their coach know? Some behaviors must be reported to the school administrator and some will require administrative action. Know which behaviors those are.

CTC Tip: To find out if educators in your building know what to report, enlist help from a colleague who works at another school site. Have them individually ask the staff, "What behavior does your building administrator expect you to report?" If the answers are consistent–Congratulations! Your procedures are working. If

137

the answers are inconsistent, work with your school's behavior team to define this more clearly. Make sure to thank your colleague and buy them a coffee!

A student's caregivers also need to be in the loop. They can be powerful partners, but they can't help if they don't know. Don't surprise the student's caregivers with a whole series of behaviors that have been escalating. Err on the side of looping them in. It can certainly be tempting to skip this communication. However, this can rob the caregiver the opportunity to recognize a pattern of behavior in their child, and can damage the trust caregivers have in us. We know how tricky these conversations can be. We have a few tricks for you in the *Framing It for Caregivers* section below.

How Teachers Close the Loop with Students

Students can be impacted by their classmates' unexpected behaviors. When a student causes a significant disruption, the teacher must decide what, if any, communication should happen with the rest of the class. This may be a time to build empathy and teach perspective-taking. We do this by explaining to students that everyone has different areas they are working on. Some students may have a harder time in math. Some may have difficulty speaking in front of their peers. Other students may find it challenging to stay regulated. When we help students acknowledge we all have areas in which to grow, they develop empathy for other students' unique challenges.

Sometimes students will ask about another student's consequences. An appropriate response might be, "Talking about other students is not something I am going to do. I will not talk about you with other students either."

If the student's behavior was extreme and they had to leave class, it is natural for the others in the room to be worried. Let them know their classmate is OK and they'll be back as soon as they are able. This is an honest answer and still preserves the student's privacy.

School Administrators Close All the Loops

When someone brings an unexpected behavior to the building administrator or dean, many people want to know how it was resolved. Be sure to circle back to the person who reported the behavior, preferably in person. Discussing student behavior is nuanced, and a lot can be lost in an email.

When getting back to the person who reported the incident, thank them for bringing the situation to you. Then, share what you can about what the student learned in the Connected Conversation. Be sure to include any relevant information about the student or the situation, whether or not there are consequences, and any additional follow-up communication that is needed. Finally, leave it open for any questions or concerns they may have. It might look this when a principal has this conversation with a teacher:

Appreciation	Ms. Wright, I appreciate you bringing this situation to me so we could partner together on supporting Chloe.
Lessons Learned	Chloe and I discussed the impact of language on others, and how using language that is not school appropriate in class is disruptive and can be interpreted as disrespectful. She acknowledges that what she did was not OK, and is anxious to make it right.

Relevant Information	Chloe shared that she is exceptionally on edge today because she was up very late last night preparing for an exam in math that has big implications for her.
Follow-up/ Consequence	Chloe is working right now on drafting a written apology to you that she will deliver in person, and is prepared to apologize to the class tomorrow, if you think that would be helpful.
Follow-up Communication	Before I walked down here, Chloe called her mom on speaker phone and told her what happened while I was listening. We let mom know that you would be sending a follow up email after you receive Chloe's apology.
Questions	Thanks again for bringing this to me. Is there anything else you think I should know, or follow up that might be helpful?

Now that you have circled back to the reporter, think about who else needs to know. Consider who is on the student's support team, how the behavior is being documented, and if you need to let someone at the district office or an outside agency know what happened. Districts have protocols for documentation and notification. If you are not sure what they are, be sure to ask, and then use them.

Keeping folks in the loop does not end at the schoolhouse doors. No one is more invested in what is going on with a student than their caregivers. How we share what happened matters. In fact, there are so many things to consider when having this conversation with a caregiver that these Connected Conversations get their own section.

Framing it for Caregivers

Who are the primary adults in a student's life? Is it Mom, Dad, Grandma, Uncle, foster parent? We call the person who provides day-to-day care for the student their "caregiver." This term is inclusive of anyone who takes care of the student and does not assume all students live with their parents.

Partnering with caregivers is a necessary and important part of our job. This partnership requires that we communicate well, and not hold back information no matter how tempting that may be. First and foremost, caregivers need to know that you care for and like their child. Every conversation, regardless of the topic, should reinforce this information. Caregivers need to hear that we care about their students out loud, just as our students do.

> *Above all, caregivers need to know*
> *we care about their child.*

The more casual conversations you can have with a student's caregivers, the better. This could be a quick conversation during drop-off or pick-up, sharing good news with a phone call, mailing positive postcards, or sending an email to brag about something great that a student did or said. If a student is working on a behavior and has a great day, celebrate that with their caregivers. These are the most fun and rewarding conversations we have.

Doing this for each and every student is not going to happen by accident. We encourage teachers and administrators to be intentional and strategic in sharing good news. Make a list of students and make a tally for every positive contact. Add "send a positive student note or phone call" to your daily to-do list. Take a few minutes, and send five happy emails home. Before leaving for the day, make a handful of positive phone calls. You will end your day feeling uplifted.

> **CTC Tip:** One of our favorite ways to ensure we send positive news home for every student is to print out address labels for the class or school, and use them to send home positive postcards until every label has been used. Then start again! We print these labels for our staff members and set aside time to write postcards at staff meetings. This is quick and easy to do, and fills the room with smiling educators.

These communications will build a culture of connection in your school community. Getting good news will make the student and caregiver's day, AND it will pave the way for any challenging conversation you may need to have down the road. It is especially important in situations when the student has a pattern of unexpected behavior. You may need to look harder for positive news to share, but that makes it all the more important. We like to think of this as making a deposit in the connected relationship bank. This ensures we have sufficient funds to draw from when we have more difficult news to share.

> **CTC Tip:** In situations where our very first encounter with a caregiver is to share an unexpected behavior, consider acknowledging that. You might try saying, "I'm so sorry the first time I'm talking with you is under these circumstances. You have such a cool kid, and I have so enjoyed getting to know them."

When sharing hard information, we again recommend a phone call over an email whenever possible. If you can, it's really helpful to make sure the caregiver knows what happened before the child leaves for the day. Our dear friend and colleague, middle school principal, Steve Ret-zlaff, taught us all about the need to frame the situation for the folks at home. When students frame the situation for their caregivers, it's not always common for them to include all the necessary bits of information. We can't really blame them!

When we have the opportunity to do the framing, there are a few things to say to the caregiver before getting into the crux of it. It's always helpful to start by assuring them that the student is physically OK, and by telling them how much we care about and like their student. It sounds like this:

> "Hi Ms. Smith, this is Erika, Chloe's Principal. She is OK, this is not an emergency; I just need to check in with you about something. She is such a kind-hearted person, and I am so glad she is a student at this school."

After you have established that their student is OK and you like and care for them, then you can talk about what happened. We recommend whenever possible that the student explains to the caregiver, in your presence, what happened. This does a couple of things. First, it increases the accountability for that student—it is often difficult for them to own up. Second, the caregiver is far less likely to argue their child could never do such a thing if they hear what happened directly from their child. Finally, when students are able to explain their actions with you present, it ensures that the student will not wiggle out of taking accountability or changing the story when they get home. Once the caregiver has the basic information, you can step in and talk about any next steps or needed follow-up.

CTC Tip: If you choose this approach, you'll want to coach the student in advance of the phone call or meeting. Make sure they know what information must be included, how to take accountability, and above all they must be honest. Practicing with the student beforehand makes sure *you* know that *they* know what to say. It also helps make them more comfortable.

If it will not work for the student to deliver the news, then after telling the caregiver how much you like and appreciate their child, be prepared to share what happened, why you think it happened that way, and what is going to happen next. If there will be a consequence, it is important to tell the caregiver that the consequence is not meant to be a punishment. The goal of the consequence is to change the behavior so the student doesn't make the same mistake again in the future.

If consequences are used as anything other than teaching tools, we need to rethink.

Encourage the caregiver to reinforce the message and the learning. Always end the conversation with a reminder that you care about their child, and thank them for teaming with you to support the student through the situation. It might sound like this:

Show Care	Hi Lila, this is Jason, Finn's teacher. This is not an emergency; Finn is fine. I just need to share something with you that happened at school today. First, I hope you know how much I appreciate Finn and all the humor and joy he brings to our class.

What happened	Today during our Science lesson, Finn got into a conflict with one of his lab partners. They disagreed with the next step and Finn shoved him hard away from the bench. The other student was OK, and did not fall, but was pretty upset. It was scary for everyone, as we were working with chemicals that can be dangerous if not handled with care.
Why you think it happened	I've noticed that Finn and the other student seem to be a bit competitive when it comes to academic achievement, and I know that Finn is feeling some pressure to maintain his grades going into finals week. When I talked to him about what happened, he seemed as surprised as I was about what he had done. He acted impulsively, and immediately regretted his actions. It was clear that if he had thought it through, he never would have put hands on the other student. It appears to be a combination of stress, impulsivity, and some pent up frustration with the other student.
What happens next	Finn and the other student have both agreed to participate in a restorative conversation tomorrow during lunch in the classroom so that the two of them can put this incident behind them. Finn will also be preparing a presentation on lab safety that he will present to me after class next week. I think this consequence will help him remember the importance of lab safety and to make safe choices in the future.

| Show Care | When Finn and I talked about this, it was obvious he made an impulsive choice, and this is not who he is. He apologized and owned up right away, which shows his strong character. I care so much about Finn and his success; I am confident that we will be able to navigate this together. Do you have any questions for me? |

Common Caregiver Stumbling Blocks

Sending your child to school is a huge act of trust, and is scary for many. Some caregivers have a history of distrust with schools, or even your school in particular. Hearing that something went wrong at school can send the best of us into defensive mode. It can be hard for a caregiver to wrap their head around their child's unexpected behaviors. As Connected Communicators, it is our job to recognize they are responding out of love and concern for their child. There are a few challenging caregiver responses that come up frequently when sharing hard news.

Caregivers respond out of love and concern for their child.

- *What about the other kid?* Caregivers are often concerned that any consequence their student is getting is the same as another student involved, regardless of different circumstances. A Connected Communicator's response is to share that we can't talk about another student, nor would we disclose information about their child. You may also have to explain that fair is not always equal, and in the same way we are considering the uniqueness of their student and what they need, we are also doing this for any other student involved. While being careful not to be too specific, it is often helpful to share what typical consequences or action steps might be when students demonstrate similar types of behaviors. This might sound like, "While I can't share exactly what I did when working with this student, I can share that when something like this occurs, we always let caregivers know and students are often home for several days."

- *My kid would never!* If you are a caregiver, you know we are often struck blind out of love for our child. It is hard to not be embarrassed or feel that it is a statement about your parenting if your child does something you are not proud of at school. Denial is an easy course to take. The best strategy in this situation is to have the student be the one to explain what they did. It is unlikely that the caregiver is going to call their own child a liar. It may be useful to say something like, "I can understand why this is so hard to wrap your head around. This seems out of character for Oliver. Nevertheless, he did make this unexpected choice this time. That is why I am calling to let you know. I think it will really help Oliver if he knows we are partnering together to support him in assuring it does not happen again."

- *You can't do this!* When a school consequence feels big to the student or family, be prepared to share school and board policy. Have your school handbook close by. This is the time to explain both the rationale, and how you are supported by policy. Offer to share a copy with them.

- *I'm going to your boss.* Connected Communicators foster relationships of trust with their boss. Sometimes caregivers let us know that they intend to go to the principal, superintendent, School Board, etc. As long as we have followed policy and done our best by the student, there is no need for us to worry. To the caregiver, simply offer to share the contact information of the appropriate person. They will see that you are not concerned they are taking it to the next level because you are confident in your actions. Always, always give your supervisor a heads-up that someone may be coming their way, along with what took place.

Connecting It: Closing the Loop

Connected Communicators make sure all of a student's team members are in the loop. It is everyone's job to make sure that caregivers are a consistent part of the student's team. This means sharing good news often, and teaming with them when a student has an unexpected behavior. When students see that we are all talking to each other, we are all on their side, and they have a team of grown-ups that care about them, it supports them in becoming the best version of themselves. When we take the time to effectively close the loop, we foster a culture of connection in our community.

Connected Takeaways

+ Support professionals should ensure the student's classroom teacher or administrator is aware of any behavior that requires follow-up.
+ Teachers should be prepared to communicate to other students after a major disruption has occurred in a way that protects privacy and re-establishes safety.
+ When administrators close the loop with the person who reported the student behavior, they can use this framework: Appreciation, Lessons Learned, Relevant Information, Follow Up/Consequence, Follow-up Communication, Questions.
+ Teachers and administrators should take care to loop in any specialist who may be working with a student (special education case manager, interventionist, school counselor, etc.).

+ Everyone on a student's support team is responsible for maintaining positive communication with families.
+ Share good news early, often, and for every student!
+ When sharing unexpected behaviors with a caregiver, use these steps: show care, what happened, why you think it happened, what happens next, end with care.
+ Be prepared for common caregiver stumbling blocks.

Welcome to the Connected Communicator Movement!

"Every child deserves a champion-an adult who will never give up on them, who understands the power of connection and insists that they become the best they can possibly be."

-Rita Pierson

In case no one has told you lately, thank you for what you do each and every day for our children. You are truly making tomorrow a better world through your dedication to lifting up the young people of our society. We are grateful for you. We are inspired by you.

What you say matters. A lot. The way that you communicate with kids has a lasting impact. Whether you are greeting them at the bus stop, serving them in the cafeteria, supervising them in the hallways or on the playground, teaching them in the classroom, or writing their tardy slips—the way in which you communicate with kids leaves a powerful impression. Your impression creates a ripple effect.

Our education community is vast. It includes folks from all walks of life, varied political affiliations, diverse backgrounds and lived experiences. What connects each of us is that we all genuinely care about kids. No matter where we are in the world, when we come together to create a culture of connection, our ripple effect is profound.

We believe deeply in the messages contained in the pages of this book, and we hope you will connect with others about the content. When we improve the way adults communicate with kids in our world, it will be revolutionary. This movement will bring our vast community together.

We invite you to explore some of the supportive tools, workshop offerings, and videos available on our website: connectingthroughconversation.com. When you read sections at staff meetings, discuss in your professional learning communities, engage in a book study, and share with other educators in your community, you will create a culture of connection. Our invitation to you is a call to connection. We hope you join us in this movement of connecting through conversation. We would love to hear from you about all the ways you are cultivating a culture of connection in your school!

If you read this book, you are looking for ways to strengthen and grow your ability to connect with students. Thank you. Thank you for joining us on this journey of making a positive difference in the lives of our students. Thank you for doing your part to make the world a better and more connected place.

Connecting It

What works best is anything that increases the quality and number of relationships in a child's life. People, not programs, change people.

-Dr. Bruce Perry

Becoming a Connected Communicator requires intentionality. The appendix includes sample scripts, sentence stems, Care Out Loud tools, and the Connected Conversation Planning Guide. These resources are designed to support you in incorporating the concepts and strategies shared in this book. These tools are also available to download from our website, www.connecting throughconversation.com. With time and practice, you too will be a Connected Communicator.

Sample Script: Elementary Playground Scuffle

Scenario

Two elementary students are playing foursquare at recess. There is a disagreement about the rules. Jose yells, "You cheated, you stupid jerk!" The playground monitor, Sandra, looks up just in time to see Ramona chuck the ball at Jose. Jose begins to cry as soon as the ball hits him squarely in the stomach. Ramona shrieks, runs off, and climbs a nearby tree. Sandra quickly assesses the situation. Jose seems hurt, but not injured. Ramona has stopped climbing, but she is still about five feet up the tree on a branch that appears to be quite stable. Sandra decides to check on Jose first. She walks over to him and finds him crying pretty hard and holding his tummy.

Connected Conversation Script

Sandra (*bending down and speaking to Jose*): Hey buddy. Wow. That really looks like it hurt, huh?
Jose (*still crying*): Yeah! It does. It hurts bad!

Sandra: I'm so sorry that hurt you, Jose. Is it only your tummy?

Jose nods.

Sandra: Ok, let's get you to the office to get some ice and get checked out.

Jose (*sniffling*): Ok.

Sandra uses her walkie-talkie to radio the office to let them know that Jose is on his way. She also asks them to send the counselor to help with Ramona. Sandra asks one of the other students to walk with Jose to the office. Sandra stays close by the tree and does her best to keep an eye on Ramona (who is still perched in the tree) and the other kids playing foursquare in the area.

The counselor, Raul, arrives and thanks Sandra for calling him over. Quickly and quietly so that Ramona can't hear the conversation, Sandra explains to Raul what happened. Sandra goes back to supervising the other students on the playground, but remains close by, in case Raul needs backup.

Raul (*calling up*): Hey, Ramona. Miss Sandra told me a little about what happened. I can see you're pretty upset and maybe looking for a place to hide. Is that why you climbed up the tree?

Ramona (*whining*): Uh huh.

Raul: Yeah, I thought that might be the case, but it's not safe to hide in that tree right now.

Ramona: But I love climbing trees.

Raul: Me too! It's super fun to climb trees. I really wish we were allowed to climb trees at school.

Ramona: I climb trees at the park, and I'm a really good climber.

Raul: It sure looks like it! But at our school, we have a rule that we can't climb trees. Why don't you come on down and we'll find a safer place to hide.

Ramona: This branch is perfect for my foot, though.

Raul: Yep. I get that. It's not super safe, though, and it's my job to make sure you're safe at school. There's a bean bag in my office that's pretty comfy and makes a great spot to hide.

Ramona looks at Raul and raises an eyebrow.

Raul: Come on over here to this branch and let's see if you need my hand to help you down.

Ramona: I got it. I don't need your help. I'm a big kid.

Raul: Cool.

Ramona makes her way down the tree and onto the ground.

Once Ramona is on the ground, Raul assesses the situation to see if Ramona is ready to talk. Ramona appears calm, but Raul doesn't want to risk Ramona climbing back up the tree. Raul knows how important it is for Ramona to understand that she can't call names and she certainly can't use physical aggression to solve problems. He determines that it would be better to have this conversation when they are inside the school and when he knows Ramona is ready to have it. He knows that it would be great for Sandra to have this conversation with Ramona as it happened right on the playground. However, she needs to be supervising this recess and the next recess, and this conversation will be a bit nuanced and take some time. Raul decides he is the best person to have a Connected Conversation with Ramona.

Raul: Hey, thanks for being a first-time listener and getting down from the tree. Let's go check out that bean bag in my office.

Ramona: OK.

Raul walks Ramona to his office and gets her set up in the bean bag.

Raul: Do you want to try this lap blanket? It's a little bit heavy and sometimes kids really like to have it on their laps to help them get calm.

Ramona: Sure. My teacher has one in her classroom, and I use it sometimes.

Raul: Cool. I'm going to give you a few minutes to get settled and chill out before we do more talking. I'll set the timer. Would you rather have 5 minutes or 7 minutes to get calm before we talk?

Ramona: How about 7?

Raul: Sure. We can do 7. If you want, you can check out this water bubble fidget and I'll come back to check in with you after that timer goes off.

Ramona sits in the bean bag and plays with the fidget. Raul checks his email and does not engage with Ramona until the timer goes off.

Raul: Hey, Ramona. How are you feeling now? Ready to talk?

Ramona: Yeah. I guess so.

Raul: I'm glad to hear that. Come on over and let's talk at the table.

Raul positions himself next to Ramona at the table.

Raul: So, Ramona? You know what I know?

Ramona: What?

Raul: I know you are a really good kid. I've known you since you were in kindergarten, and you've always been a really good kid.

Ramona looks down.

Raul: And even really good kids make mistakes. Even really good grown-ups make mistakes.

Ramona: Uh huh.

Raul: I think today you made some mistakes.

Ramona: Yeah.

Raul: OK. Let's talk about it. Can you tell me what happened at recess with Jose? It seems like you were pretty upset with him.

Ramona: I was! He totally cheated at foursquare.

Raul: And that made you mad.

Ramona: Super mad! Infinity mad.

Raul: Why were you infinity mad?

Ramona: BECAUSE HE CHEATED!

Raul takes a deep breath, looks away, and pauses for a few moments.

Raul (*in a calm and quiet voice*): Right, you were infinity mad because he cheated.

Ramona (*quieter, but still upset*): Yes! That's what I just said!

Raul: I hear you. You were infinity mad because he cheated.

Ramona (*quiet and more calm now*): Yeah.

Raul: Can you tell me what he did that was cheating?

Ramona: He did a double bounce and hit the line. I told him he was out, and then he cherry bombed it in my square, and then he said I was out! But he was out first. It wasn't fair.

Raul: Oh my. That doesn't sound fair.

Ramona: It wasn't fair. He is such a cheater. A total cheat.

Raul: He didn't play by the rules and you got mad.

Ramona: Uh huh.

Raul: I get that. You wanted to play and you wanted it to be fair. When he did the double bounce and it hit the line, he should have been out.

Ramona: Yep. He should have been out. Not me.

Raul: Right. But when he called you out, you got super mad.

Ramona: Uh huh.

Raul: And then you threw the ball at him.

Ramona: But it wasn't on purpose. I accidentally threw the ball at him.

Raul: Hmm . . . well . . . (*pauses for a moment*) That's not really an accident. An accident is if you *accidentally* bump into someone or *accidentally* drop something. You didn't *accidentally* throw the ball at Jose.

Ramona grunts.

Raul: Ramona, you know what I think?

Ramona: What?

Raul: I don't think you stopped and thought about what you were doing before you threw the ball. I think you threw the ball without thinking, and then you wished you hadn't done it.

Ramona: Well . . . I guess . . . Yeah.

Raul: Yeah. So that's not an accident, but you did it and then wished you hadn't done it.

Ramona nods.

Raul: Did you mean to hurt Jose when you threw the ball?

Ramona: No way! I was just mad.

Raul: Infinity mad and you didn't stop and think?

Ramona: Yeah.

Raul: And you didn't mean to hurt him?

Ramona: No, I really didn't. I was mad, but I did not want him to get hurt.

Raul: And then you wished you hadn't thrown it at him?

Ramona: Yeah. I really wish I hadn't thrown it.

Raul: Is that why you ran and climbed up the tree?

Ramona nods.

Raul: Yeah. You know we can't run away and climb trees at our school, right?

Ramona: I know.

Raul: Why not?

Ramona: Cuz I could fall and get hurt?

Raul: Exactly. Can you let me know that you won't climb the tree at school again?

Ramona: I won't climb the tree at school.

Raul: Thank you. I really appreciate your promise. Let's make a plan for next time so you know where you can take a break. We'll need to find a safe place because up in the tree isn't safe at school.

Ramona: OK.

Raul: Where do you think could work?

Ramona: To hide?

Raul: Well. Not exactly. Where do you think it could work for you to take a break when you are outside during recess? It has to be in-bounds and the grown-ups need to be able to see you.

Ramona: What about the bench?

Raul: The one by the big rocks?

Ramona: Yes.

Raul: I think that could work. It's in bounds, but a little bit away, and the grown-ups can still see you there. Yes, that does work. Do you think you could remember to go there when you need a break?

Ramona: Yeah.

Raul: Great! You and I can make a plan later about *when* to take a break too.

Ramona: OK.

Raul: Thanks. So we need to talk about what you did to Jose.

Ramona: Do we have to?

Raul: Yeah, kiddo. We do.

Ramona: OK.

Raul: I wonder how Jose felt when you threw the ball at him?

Ramona: Probably confused.

Raul: Right. I bet he did feel confused. I wonder what else he might have felt?

Ramona: I dunno.

Raul: I wonder if he felt scared.

Ramona: Probably. And maybe hurt too?

Raul: Yep. I bet he felt all those things. Confused, scared, and hurt. He could have really gotten hurt. Right now he's in the office and his tummy is really hurting. When you hit him with the ball, he started crying pretty hard.

Ramona: I didn't mean to hurt him.

Raul: I know you didn't *mean* to hurt him. You did, though.

Ramona (*very quietly*): I know.

Raul: Yeah. It's hard when we do something and it hurts someone and that wasn't what we meant to do. Isn't it?

Ramona: Yeah. I wish I didn't do that.

Raul: Yeah, me too. Even though you wish you hadn't done it and you didn't mean to hurt him, you did.

Ramona's eyes well up with tears.

Raul stays quiet for a few moments and sits in the silence, allowing Ramona to Sit in the Fire.

Raul: Are you feeling sad about that?

Ramona: Uh huh.

Raul: I can tell.

Ramona starts to cry a little. Raul gets her a tissue and gives her some time.

Raul: Hey Ramona? You are a good kid and you made a mistake. You did something without thinking, and now you feel sad about it.

Ramona nods.

Raul: Yeah. It doesn't feel good when we hurt someone.

Ramona nods.

Raul: So now, our job is to do what we can to help make it better. We need to figure out how to remember to use our words and not throw things when we are mad. (Pauses) Next time what can you do when you are super mad?

Ramona: I dunno.

Raul: Do you want to throw a ball at someone again?

Ramona: No!

Raul: Oh, good! I'm glad to hear you want to make a change. (*Pauses*) So I wonder what we can do differently when you are super mad?

Ramona: I don't know.

Raul: Remember how we talk about stop, think, and make a good choice?

Ramona: Yeah!

Raul: OK! So what could you do next time you are mad - *before* you throw something?

Ramona: I could stop and think and make a good choice?

Raul: Exactly! You could stop and think. When you remember to stop and think, you usually make pretty good choices.

Ramona: Yep.

Raul: I wonder what a good choice might be next time?

Ramona: I could walk away.

Raul: You could walk away! Where might you go?

Ramona: To the bench maybe.

Raul: That sounds like a great idea! Could you also maybe talk to a grown-up?

Ramona: Yeah.

Raul: Who could you talk to?

Ramona: Miss Sandra or my teacher.

Raul: That would totally work.

Ramona: OK.

Raul: Hmmm . . . I wonder if there is something that you could do to help Jose feel better?

Ramona: But he did cheat!

Raul: Right. It's not OK to cheat. I agree. I'll be sure to talk to Jose about the foursquare rules. I can also review the rules with all the kids so that we don't have any confusion about what the rules are and who makes the calls.

Ramona: Really?

Raul: For sure. But, Ramona, even though you thought Jose cheated, is it OK to throw a ball at someone when you are mad?

Ramona (*looking down*): No.

Raul: So I wonder what you could do to help make it better?

Ramona: I guess I could say sorry.

Raul: I think that might help Jose feel better. I also think that it could help repair your friendship. Are you ready to do that now?

Ramona: Yeah, I am.

Raul: Thanks, Ramona. That will make a big difference.

After the Conversation

Raul will need to close this loop after the conversation. He'll need to consult his administrator about any further consequences for Ramona and he'll need to follow up with Jose. It will also be important to connect with Ramona's teacher, as well as Sandra who reported the situation. Raul will have to consider who should make the call home to inform Jose and Ramona's caregivers. He also promised to make sure someone reviews foursquare rules with the students. Finally, he might make a plan to meet with Ramona (when she is not escalated or debriefing an incident) to discuss and practice using individualized regulation strategies to use when she is escalated or dysregulated.

Common Student Move: Fleeing

Ramona has used fleeing as a strategy in the past. Because of this, Raul uses strategic positioning to make sure she stays with him as they change location.

Connected Communicator Moves

Sandra used her quick thinking, and what she knows about planning the conversation, to determine who should take what role in handling the situation. She also uses Acknowledge, Validate, Coach with Jose.

Raul also makes extensive use of Acknowledge, Validate, Coach throughout the conversation he had with Ramona. He is thoughtful of how to plan for the conversation in determining the where, when, and who in both the conversation and the follow-up. Throughout the conversation, Raul stays grounded and maintains the calm he wants Ramona to also show. He avoids a power struggle by using an "I wish" statement when talking her down from the tree. Did you notice how he didn't ask any questions of Ramona when he was trying to get her to leave the tree? Later he offers choice when he asks how many minutes she needs to get calm. He chooses when not to talk strategically, allowing her to de-escalate by giving her time in a new location with calming tools and a timer. He also employs silence later in the conversation when he allows her to Sit in the Fire and reflect on how she hurt Jose.

Throughout the conversation, Raul positions himself strategically for both safety and to increase Ramona's comfort. He does not ask her to make eye contact, and does not sit or stand directly across from her.

He employs COLBA, making sure that Ramona knows she is cared for. There is significant teaching that Raul does in this conversation, including teaching Ramona the difference between an impulse and a choice, the difference between an accident and regretting an action done on impulse, and that intention does not negate impact. Through his questioning techniques, he guides Ramona to come to many of these learnings herself. Raul doesn't lose his cool and he doesn't take her behavior personally.

Sample Script: Middle School Cafeteria Argument

Scenario

Two middle school students are in the cafeteria. They are loudly arguing over the last chair at a table. As the school principal, Mr. Brooks, walks over, he overhears Jasmine yell at Sam, "Shut up and go away, you immature, stupid loser. No one wants to sit with you."

Connected Conversation Script

Mr. Brooks: Whoa. Jasmine, we don't talk like that about our classmates at Whitford Middle School. You can take your lunch to my office and I will be there in a few minutes to check in with you.

Jasmine: What?! That's not fair, she's the one who keeps butting into our group.

Mr. Brooks (*in a calm but firm tone*): OK, sounds like we have some things to talk about. It is important to me that I understand what is going on, and I want to make sure I can listen to all you have to tell me. Head to my office, I'll be right behind you.

Jasmine: Whatever, this is so stupid. (*She stomps off in the direction of the office.*)

Mr. Brooks: Sam, go ahead and put your tray down, I just want to chat with you quickly for a minute.

Sam (*With tears now running down her face, she silently puts down her tray and follows Mr. Brooks to an empty table*): It is not a big deal, I don't want Jasmine to be in trouble-she will just be more mad at me.

Mr. Brooks: I get that you don't want your friend to get in trouble, that makes sense. I will tell her that you didn't want her to get in trouble if that will help, but I can see you are really upset. I'm thinking that what Jasmine said hurt your feelings? Is that right?

Sam: Yeah. It was really mean. I just don't want her to be mad at me anymore.

Mr. Brooks: I totally get that. Tell me more about what is going on.

Sam: I don't know, Jasmine and I used to be good friends. All of a sudden, she doesn't want me around. She keeps inviting friends to do things and telling them not to tell me, and now she wouldn't let me sit with everyone at lunch. They are my friends too! I don't really want to sit with Jasmine anymore, but all my friends are with her. I can't be by myself at lunch, that would be so embarrassing. I don't know what to do!

Sam is still crying softly.

Mr. Brooks (*handing Sam a tissue*): I am so sorry. It is so hard when we get excluded, especially by someone who is a friend and we don't know why.

Sam: Well, it's because I'm immature. I don't want to do some of the things they want to do. I don't know why I have to be such a baby all the time.

Mr. Brooks: Sam, it takes a very mature person to say no to something they don't feel comfortable doing when all of their friends are doing it.

The most important thing is to do what is right for you. This shows what a mature person you are. You don't need to tell me what kind of things you are talking about, but I'm wondering if your mom would be proud of the decision you made to say no.

Sam: Yeah. She would be. But she doesn't get it-everyone else wanted to. I was just scared to get in trouble.

Mr. Brooks: Sam, I know your mom. She is a smart lady, and I know it is hard to believe, but she was thirteen once. I am so impressed by you for sticking by what you knew was right, and putting more importance on what your mom expects of you than your friends. That is really, really hard, especially when you are in middle school. You are such a smart young lady, and I know you are fun to be around as well. Talk about the rest of your friends at that table. Is it just Jasmine, or were other people giving you a hard time?

Sam (*calmer now and no longer crying*): It is really just Jasmine. Everyone else just looks away and ignores it when she's mean to me.

Mr. Brooks: OK, do you feel like you want to go eat with them then, or do you want to have a quiet space to eat today?

Sam: I want to eat with my friends, but what do I say when I go back?

Mr. Brooks: I think the best thing to do is try and brush it off for now. It would be OK to say something like "that was stupid" and then just start eating. Does that feel OK?

Sam: Yeah, I think so. It's OK to say it was stupid?

Mr. Brooks: Yep, you have my permission to say this situation is stupid.

Sam: OK. Please don't get Jasmine in trouble. I don't want things to get worse!

Mr. Brooks: I totally get that. Remember, Jasmine is responsible for her choices, just like you are responsible for yours. I'll make sure she knows you did not want her to get into trouble.

Sam: OK.

Sam walks back to her friends.

Mr. Brooks watches her sit down. He observes the conversation from a distance until he feels confident that the others at the table seem welcoming. Mr. Brooks then goes to the office to talk to Jasmine. Jasmine is sitting at the round table in his office under the watchful eye of the secretary. Mr. Brooks takes a seat next to Jasmine so they are at roughly a ninety degree angle to each other.

Mr. Brooks: You seemed pretty upset with Sam. What's going on?

Jasmine: Ugh. Nothing! She's just such a loser and she is always trying to hang out with us. I didn't do anything!

Mr. Brooks: I want to hear more so it is important that we don't call her names while we figure this out. I wouldn't let anyone call you a loser. I'm wondering if something has changed? It has always seemed to me that you two were good friends.

Jasmine: Whatever. Well, we were friends. But we aren't anymore.

Mr. Brooks: Did something happen?

Jasmine: No, she's just so immature and doesn't like to do the same things we do.

Mr. Brooks: People can like to do different things, and still be friends. Especially when they have things like school and band in common.

Jasmine: Right, but I don't want to be her friend-she's a los... (*Mr. Brooks interrupts*)

Mr. Brooks: I want you to think before you finish that sentence. Remember, we are not going to call anyone names. That's not how we do things here.

Jasmine (*rolling her eyes*): Whatever. I don't want to be friends. She thinks she is so much better than us just because . . .well whatever, I don't want to talk about it. You can't make us be friends.

Mr. Brooks: You're right. I can't make you be friends with Sam. However, it is my job to make sure we are always kind to each other at school. Tell me more about what you meant when you said, "No one wants to sit with you". Tell me about that.

Jasmine: Ugh. I know that wasn't nice. It's true, though. They think she's immature too.

Mr. Brooks: Well, true or not, I want you to imagine how you would feel if someone said that to you. Especially about a group of people that have been your friends for a long time.

Jasmine: Well, it wouldn't be true if someone said that to me. She is just trying to get me in trouble. I hate her!

Mr. Brooks: Actually, she was very concerned that you would get in trouble. She told me more than once that she did not want you to get in trouble for this. Hate is a very strong word. It is surprising that you would have such strong feelings if nothing happened. Are you sure there isn't a disagreement or something that happened that you want to tell me about?

Jasmine: No. It's none of your business. Why? Did she say something?

Mr. Brooks: Nope, I'm just trying to understand. What do you think she would have told me about?

Jasmine: Ugh. I don't know! It doesn't matter. Can I go back to lunch now?

Mr. Brooks: Nope. You called another student an unkind name, and you were trying to exclude her from sitting at the table at lunch. You don't have to be friends, but you do have to be kind. At Whitford it is not OK to call people names, and it is not OK to exclude people. Although Sam didn't want you to get in trouble, it was very clear to me that she was upset. Her feelings were really hurt. I know my feelings would be hurt if someone called me names and said no one wants to sit with me. What you said goes against our school agreements.

Jasmine looks down.

Mr. Brooks: Jasmine, I know you are a kind person, I have seen you show so much kindness here at school. Even kind people sometimes do something that they later realize was really unkind. The most important thing to do when that happens is to take responsibility and make it right. I am going to go back to the cafeteria. You can hang out here and finish your lunch. When I come back, we are going to have to figure out what we can do to make this right.

Jasmine: But, I didn't do anything!

Mr. Brooks: Sounds like you have some thinking to do. I'll be back.

Mr. Brooks leaves the office and asks the secretary to keep an eye on Jasmine through the open door. He returns 10 minutes later.

Mr. Brooks: When I left, you were confused about why I was needing to talk to you about what happened at lunch. Have you had a chance to think about why I'm concerned?

Jasmine: Well, I know I called Sam a name, but she deserved it!

Mr. Brooks: I don't believe anyone deserves to be called names. It seems like you are really angry with Sam. You don't need to tell me why, but I know your dad, and he is going to want to know what is going on. We are going to have to call him and fill him in. When we do, I want to be able to say that you understand what you did was not in alignment with the Whitford Way, and are ready to take responsibility. I don't think we are there yet. Do you need more time?

Jasmine (*now crying*): You can't tell my dad! I didn't even do anything. He is going to be so mad. Please don't tell him!

Mr. Brooks: We don't keep secrets from parents here. Why is he going to be mad if you didn't do anything?

Jasmine: I know I called her a name. He won't like that. He's friends with Sam's dad.

Mr. Brooks: I'm glad you see that calling someone a name is not OK. What else happened that is not in alignment with the Whitford Way?

Jasmine: I don't know, it's not my fault if no one else wants to sit with her either.

Mr. Brooks: OK, you need more time. Remember, we don't exclude people at Whitford. I'm going to let Mrs. Johnson know you will be late to P.E. While I'm gone, I want you to think about what happened that is not in alignment with the Whitford Way. All of it. Then we can figure out where to go from here.

Jasmine puts her head down, clearly upset. Mr. Brooks leaves the office. He returns about five minutes later. Jasmine's head is still on the table.

Mr. Brooks: I can see you are not ready. I will know you are ready when you lift your head off the table.

Mr. Brooks goes to the computer and starts going through some e-mail, glancing up consistently to see if Jasmine lifts her head up. After about five minutes, she lifts her head.

Mr. Brooks: Thanks for letting me know you are ready. Can you tell me now how what happened is not in alignment with the Whitford way?

Jasmine: I was mean to Sam. I called her a name, and I made her think no one wants to be her friend.

Mr. Brooks: That's right. Thanks for acknowledging that Jasmine, I'm proud of you for owning up. That is hard when we have made a mistake. Let's think about where to go from here. How are we going to make this right with Sam?

Jasmine: I don't know. I really don't want to be her friend anymore.

Mr. Brooks: That's OK, you don't have to be her friend. We just have to make sure we are always treating people with respect and kindness. Did you do that here?

Jasmine: No

Mr. Brooks: OK, so how can we make that right?

Jasmine: I guess I could say I'm sorry.

Mr. Brooks: That's a good start. I think an apology that is real would be meaningful. I'm not sure it is enough to make sure this conflict doesn't continue. It seems to me that we might need to have a conversation with her about that. Do you remember when we did a classroom circle in Mrs. Jones' class to problem solve the issue we were having with taking care of the art supplies?

Jasmine: Yeah, I think so.

Mr. Brooks: What would you think about having a conversation like that one with the three of us? You can apologize, and hear how your words and actions impacted Sam. We can also talk about how we can be in school together and treat each other with respect and kindness even if we are not going to be good friends anymore.

Jasmine: Ugh. That is so embarrassing. Do I have to?

Mr. Brooks: No, you don't have to. The alternative would be to apologize and have a supervised lunch for a period of time so we can make sure something like this does not happen again. What sounds better to you?

Jasmine: I guess I want to do the circle thing.

Mr. Brooks: Great, I think that is a solid choice. I will check in with Sam and make sure she is open to it. Now we need to let your dad know what is going on. I'm going to have you make that phone call. I will be listening, so it is really important that you are honest, and tell him the whole story. I think one of the reasons you are nervous about telling your dad is he is going to want to know why you and Sam are not friends any more. You don't need to have that conversation in front of me, but you are going to need to think about how you are going to talk to your dad about this. I am going to recommend that you are totally honest with him. He loves you and he wants to help. Ready to make the call?

Jasmine: Can't I just tell him tonight, why do we have to call him now? He's at work!

Mr. Brooks: If he can't answer, we can leave a message. It is important that we let him know now. You can hang out in my office until you are ready.

Jasmine: Fine. Let's just call.

Mr. Brooks dials dad's number and he picks up.

Mr. Brooks: Hi Mr. Rosiliz, this is Mr. Brooks. There is no emergency, but Jasmine has something she needs to tell you. Before she does, I just want to let you know how impressed I am of her willingness to be honest with me and take accountability for what happened at lunch today. She is a wonderful young lady who made a mistake. I'm sure we can work it through together. I'm going to hand the phone to Jasmine to let you know what is going on.

After the Conversation

After Jasmine lets her dad know what happened, Mr. Brooks lets her dad know that she missed lunch today, and will be having a restorative conversation to make amends with Sam tomorrow. He also encourages him to find out more about whatever took place that has caused Jasmine to decide that Sam is "immature", as he is pretty sure this is at the heart of that matter. He also shares that it involved Sam saying no to doing something that Jasmine wanted to do, and that whatever that thing was, Jasmine felt it was none of Mr. Brook's business and it is the reason she now thinks Sam is "immature." He shared with her dad that as the principal he does not need to know, but as her dad, he would for sure want to know. The dad thanks him, and assures him he will be finding out what is really going on. Mr. Brooks also follows up by calling Sam's mom to let her know what happened, and encourages her to find out more.

Mr. Brooks also closes the loop with Sam and Jasmine's seventh period teacher as this is the only class they have in common. He cautions both girls to stay away from each other at school and on social media until they have the restorative conversation the next day.

Common Student Move: Denial

In this case, Mr. Brooks is able to ignore Jasmine's denial, as he witnessed the behavior. It became more about helping Jasmine to see that calling students a name and excluding them is not "nothing" no matter how justified you feel. This helped to avoid a power struggle.

He referred to these things as being against the Whitford Way. Referring to your code of conduct or school values is always helpful.

Connected Communicator Moves

Mr. Brooks was careful to avoid a power struggle with Jasmine by not asking questions when there wasn't a question, and removing the audience. He was thoughtful in planning the who, what, where, and when of the conversations with both Jasmine and Sam. He Cared Out Loud for both students. He was careful to acknowledge and validate their feelings before coaching, utilizing the acknowledge, validate, coach technique. He did not get sidetracked into whatever issue started their disagreement in the first place, and stayed focused on the issue at hand. He allowed Jasmine to *Sit in the Fire*, and employed the ready/not-ready technique. He used silence and time alone strategically. He provided choice where he could, making sure he could live with either outcome. He closed the loop with parents and teachers so all could be on the same page. He went a step further with the parents by letting them know that something occurred that they should look more into, but stayed in his lane regarding the behavior at school. This causes the parents to consider him on their team. Throughout the conversation, Mr. Brooks was calm and kind. He was demonstrating the emotions he wanted these students to catch from him.

Sample Script:
High School Plagiarism

Scenario

An eleventh-grade language arts teacher, Ms. McCarthy, realizes that, Julia, one of the students in her class, has plagiarized an essay. In preparation for the conversation, the teacher has printed out the Wikipedia article and the essay the student handed in as her own. While students are independently working, Ms. McCarthy taps Julia on the shoulder, and asks her to chat in the hallway. Ms. McCarthy stands with her back to the wall and motions for Julia to stand next to her.

Ms. McCarthy: Hey, Julia, I just wanted to check in because I care about you. You are such an important member of our classroom community. I need to let you know that I was reading your essay last night, and I noticed that it was written in a style different from what I am used to seeing from you. I'm wondering if there is anything that you want to tell me.

Julia: Nope.

Ms. McCarthy: Huh. It was really unusual. Are you sure?

Julia: Yep.

Ms. McCarthy: (*Long pause*) Hmmm ... That's a little confusing to me. Take a look at this (*shows student the 2 printed documents*) Your essay and this Wikipedia article look similar. In fact, they are identical in most areas. Can you help me understand why that might be?

Julia: (*Deep breath*) OK. OK. So ... The truth is I wrote that article and posted it on Wikipedia.

Ms. McCarthy: Wow. Huh. Wow. That is just so unexpected. (*Deep breath and recenter*) Julia, I've always considered you a person who works to uphold our community's value of integrity. Of course, even people with a lot of integrity make mistakes sometimes. Anytime someone makes a mistake and then takes responsibility for it, it's a lot easier to make a repair and restore their integrity. You know, I'm going to check back in on our class, why don't you take a minute and just think about what should tell me.

Ms. McCarthy leaves for 5 minutes. Julia waits in the hall, Sitting in the Fire.

Ms. McCarthy: So, Julia. What do you think? Are you feeling ready to share what is going on?

Julia (*Looking at the ground*): This was super hard. I really tried to write it, but then I got stuck, and then I had practice, and I was scared. I knew that if I didn't turn this in, I would not be eligible to play this weekend so I copied it from Wikipedia.

Ms. McCarthy: I'm so glad you told me that. I heard you say that it was really stressful and hard for you. I know how important volleyball is to you and I can imagine you must have felt a lot of pressure. That took real courage to admit your mistake. Thank you for showing your integrity and telling me the truth. What do you think you can do to make this right?

After the Conversation:

Ms. McCarthy is going to have to follow school policy and determine how to respond to Julia's academic dishonesty. She will communicate with Julia's volleyball coach and her parents. Depending on school policy, she may also alert building administration and ensure the behavior is recorded.

Common Student Move: Denial

When a student denies the behavior that they clearly did, the best response is to present all of the reasons you are struggling to believe them, and then give space as the teacher did here. Ms. McCarthy also utilized COLBA and reminded her that the most important thing to do when you have made a mistake is take accountability.

Connected Communicator Moves

Ms. McCarthy had obviously prepared for the conversation, thinking through the best place to have the conversation, how to position herself, and printing out the documents to use as the third point. She set up the conversation by leaning on the already established relationship, and reminding the student of their critical part of the classroom community. She then gave the student plenty of room to tell the truth, without directly accusing her of anything, choosing to not talk and avoid any power struggle. She also made sure to give space between any action and the students character, by using COLBA.

Walking away and giving the student time to Sit in the Fire were critical moves in this communication, allowing the student to both think and save face. The teacher's reaction showed active listening, continued care, and gave credit to the student taking responsibility. The teacher both offered appreciation for the students courage in doing the right thing, without letting them off the hook to take accountability.

APPENDIX D

Sentence Stems for Connected Communicators

To Show Authentic Listening:

+ "I think I am hearing you say... Did I get that right?"
+ "Let me make sure I have this right..."
+ "Can you help me make sure I understand? Are you saying...?"

Determining the Function of a Behavior:

+ "Tell me a little about what happened."
+ "What were you thinking about or feeling when it happened?"
+ "Tell me more about what's going on."
+ "What was going on for you right before that happened?"
+ "What were you hoping would happen?"

Getting to Know Younger Students:

+ What's your favorite part of the day?
+ If you could wish for three things, what would they be?

- What is something that cheers you up when you are sad?
- What do you think is the best part of being a grown-up? Being a kid?
- If you could eat only one food for the rest of your life, what would it be?
- If you had a magic wand, what is the first thing you would do with it?
- What is something you are really good at?
- What is the funniest joke you know?

Getting to Know Older Students:

- What is your favorite after-school activity? What do you like about it?
- What school rule do you wish would be eliminated? Why?
- What are you most proud of?
- What kind of movies do you like to watch? Why?
- If you had to pick just one cause to fight for, which one would it be?
- What advice would you give to adults about how to make the world a better place by the time you are an adult?
- What is most exciting about what comes after high school? What do you find most stressful about it?
- What advice do you have for students getting ready to start at the high school/middle school?

Caring Out Loud

- I care about you.
- You're awesome!
- I'm so glad you are here.
- This class is better because you are in it.

+ Your success is important to me, because you are important to me.
+ You matter.
+ You're a rock star!
+ I am so impressed by you
+ I am so glad you are in this class/on this bus/on this team at our school.
+ You are such a cool kid!

To Encourage Student Reflection: Sitting in the Fire:

+ I can see you are having some big feelings. That's really normal and understandable. It seems like maybe you wish you might have done something differently. I wonder what that might be?
+ Oh wow - that was kind of a big deal. How are you feeling about this now?
+ Hmmm . . . that really hurt your classmate's feelings. Was that your intention?

Examining Intention vs Impact:

+ I understand it wasn't your intention, however, the impact of your actions caused . . .
+ I get that's not what you meant, but it made them feel . . .
+ I know you didn't mean to, but their feelings are really hurt.

Avoiding Power Struggles:

+ I care about you too much to argue.
+ I'll talk to you when your voice sounds like mine.

+ "This is important, and I want to discuss it with you. We are going to have to wait until we are both feeling calmer. Let's circle back to this towards the end of class."
+ Avoid asking a question if there isn't a choice! Use "You can" or "You may" statements (e.g., You can take a seat, you may get a pencil).
+ Use diffusers: "I hear you," "Good point," "Noted"
+ "I need your help. What ideas do you have to fix this problem?"
+ "This is an important discussion. Let's connect on a solution that will work for both of us after class."
+ "I wish. . ." (that you could do that thing, or didn't have to do that thing)
+ "Well. . . that was unexpected."

Connected Conversation Planning Guide Template

Who: Who is best positioned to have this conversation? If it is you, what do you already know or need to know about the student to facilitate the conversation?

What: Describe the purpose of the conversation. What are some key ideas or talking points that must be communicated?

Where: What level of privacy is required?

When: Are you emotionally and physically ready? How much time do you need? How urgent is the conversation? Consider the impact on student learning.

Care Out Loud Strategies

Intentionally greet each student when they arrive: This can be as simple as greeting students with a smile and saying, "Hi Jamar, I am so glad to see you today." If you can be near the bus loop, or in the hallway in front of the classroom to welcome students as they arrive, do it. If you are the bus driver, you are setting the tone for the day. This serves more than one purpose. Students feel valued when we greet them by name, and we notice that we feel more connected all day long.

Say an individual goodbye as students leave: Taking the time to end class with a positive exchange can make all the difference. The first and last things we hear stick with us the longest. Take advantage of this by using this time to remind students you care about them. Student pick up areas are great places to build relationships with students and their families. Get out there and say goodbye.

Get to know students using writing or interviewing: Many teachers have students write a letter introducing themselves to the teacher, or some version of this at the start of the year. With younger students, using interviews, surveys, or drawings can also be effective ways to get to know your students right away. Consider the following writing or interview prompts:

- ✦ What is something you would like me to know about you?
- ✦ Tell me about the people you live with.
- ✦ What helps you learn best?
- ✦ What are you good at? What's hard for you?

Keep the conversation going: When we ask students to write to us, we make sure to write back. This is a great opportunity to provide personalized feedback on what makes them awesome. Make as many connections as you can to what they shared about themselves. For example, "It is so cool that you like to swim; I have always loved to be in the water." You might want to develop a system for keeping track of these tidbits so you can refer to them later when you need to break the ice.

Provide meaningful praise on their work and their progress: Sharing with them how impressed you are of their growth and accomplishments will fill students with pride. This will also make it more likely they'll keep it up.

Celebrate their birthdays—no matter how old they are: We are never too old to appreciate being wished a happy birthday. Before the year starts, make sure each student's birthday is calendared, either publicly or on your own calendar, and establish a birthday tradition. In the classroom, maybe the student gets a small prize and the class sings happy birthday. Maybe the birthday student selects part of the lesson for that day. Maybe you all get a small treat. At the school level, share birthdays over the loudspeaker, have a monthly birthday lunch bunch, or send a positive note home to the birthday student's family. If you have a digital reader board, add birthday students to the running announcements.

Whatever it is, the key piece is to acknowledge their special day, and let them know we are glad they were born.

Give them choice and ownership in their education: Wherever we can provide students choice, we should. Are there different ways to demonstrate their learning for a particular standard? Could there be a vote on an important decision for the class or school? What if the class works together to establish classroom agreements? How could a school administrator or teacher use classroom circles to gather information about an important decision? This is their education, and we want them to know it belongs to them.

Ask for feedback and use it: When we ask students for feedback, it lets them know we care what they think because we honor and respect them. Get feedback early and often, and share with them how you will use it. This means you need the information *before* the school year ends.

Responses to Common Student Move: Denial

Help Me Help You: Remind them that you are on their side. Always. Let them know that you really want to help them figure this out, but you can't help them if they are not being honest with you.

Lay Out the Evidence: If you know this student did the thing, lay out all of the reasons you know this. If it was reported by another educator, ask why they would lie about something like this. It is a good idea to start with something like, "I'm confused because I was told or I saw this behavior and you are telling me something different. Help me understand."

Take Your Time: This is a good time to allow students to think it through. Saying something like, "It is clear you need some time to consider how to best tell me what is going on. I'm going to leave you here to think about what you want to tell me. While you are thinking, remember that we all make mistakes, and the only way forward is to be honest and take responsibility." This is also a good time to indicate that in some way you are going to gather some additional evidence. For example, "I'm going to go check with Ms. Julie, because what you are telling me and what she told me are different."

Give an Out: Students are now struggling with the fact that they told you a lie on top of whatever the behavior is. Saying something like, "I can understand why you might have been nervous about being honest with me. It takes a lot of courage to admit when you have made a mistake. When we talk to your parents about this, I want to be able to say that you took responsibility. I am giving you another opportunity to be completely honest."

Lay Out the Consequences: *Lay Out the Consequences:* When a student is not being honest, explain the consequences for the original infraction, as well as additional consequences for dishonesty. Explain that their lack of integrity and any time spent on additional investigation and the lack of integrity will be considered when determining next steps. You might say, "Well, it seems like I have more investigating to do. I am going to talk to all the other witnesses involved. This will take me a lot of time, and that's OK *if* you are telling the truth. It's really important for you to know if the results of my investigation indicate that you are not being honest with me, there will be additional consequences. Before I do that, I want to give you another opportunity to tell the whole truth now."

Apologizing after an ASLO

Acknowledge that a mistake was made: Make it clear what you are apologizing for. Name the action and when it happened.

Express regret that it happened: This is the literal apology. Most of the time this means saying "I'm sorry" or "I apologize."

Vow not to be a repeat offender: If you apologize and then turn around and do it again, it will seem as though you weren't genuinely sorry. Only apologize if you intend to change the behavior, otherwise it will further erode trust. If, despite your best intentions, you find yourself repeating the behavior, you will need to do some deeper reflection to understand why so you can change moving forward.

Guess at how it made them feel: Take a guess and what kind of impact your actions may have had on the student. Saying something like "I imagine you might have felt. . . when I . . ." should do the trick.

Check in to see if you got it right: By letting them know you understand what they are feeling, you are demonstrating their feelings are valid and important.

Make it right: Ask the student if there is anything you can do to repair the situation or rebuild trust. Then do that thing!

References

Brookfield, S. D. (2015). *The skillful teacher : on technique, trust, and responsiveness in the classroom*. (3rd ed.). Jossey-Bass.

Brown, B., Fortgang, L., & Audible, I. (2015). *The gifts of imperfection*. Tullamarine, Victoria] Bolinda Audio.

Cobb, F., & Krownapple, J. (2019). *Belonging through a culture of dignity : the keys to successful equity implementation*. Mimi & Todd Press.

Covey, S. M. R. (2006). *The speed of trust : why trust is the ultimate determinant of success or failure in your relationships, career, and life*. Simon & Schuster.

Four reasons why eye contact can cause brain overstimulation. (2020, April 5). The Functional Neurology Center. https://thefnc.com/research/four-reasons-why-eye-contact-can-cause-brain-overstimulation/

Greene, R. W. (2014). *Lost at school : why our kids with behavioral challenges are falling through the cracks and how we can help them*. Scribner.

Gross, D. A. (2014, July 31). *This Is Your Brain on Silence*. Nautilus. https://nautil.us/this-is-your-brain-on-silence-235023/

Hammond, Z. (2015). *Culturally responsive teaching and the brain: Promoting authentic engagement and rigor among culturally and linguistically diverse students*. Corwin.

The Impact of Secondary Trauma on Educators. (n.d.). ASCD. https://www.ascd.org/el/articles/the-impact-of-secondary-trauma-on-educators

Lavezzi , M. (2015). *Stop, Think and Make Good Choices* . Melania Lavezzi .

Lipton, L. & Wellman B, (2022). *Learning-Focused Supervision* (2nd ed.). Miravia, LLC.

Mehrabian, A. (1971). *Silent messages : implicit communication of emotions and attitudes*. Wadsworth Pub. Co.

Raynolds, N. (2017). *Transforming Your Inner Critic Into an Inner Coach*. Createspace Independent Publishing Platform.

Reframing Classroom Management: A toolkit for educators. (n.d.). Retrieved February 12, 2023, from https://www.learningforjustice.org/sites/default/files/general/TT_Reframing_Classroom_Managment_Handouts.pdf

Riordan, R. (2010). *The red pyramid.* Disney/Hyperion.

Romero, V. E., Robertson, R., & Warner, A. (2018). *Building resilience in students impacted by adverse childhood experiences : a whole-staff approach.* Corwin.

Rosenberg, M. B. (2015). *Nonviolent Communication: A Language of Life* (3rd ed.). Puddledancer Press.

The Subtle Dance of Eye Contact in Conversation | Psychology Today. (n.d.). Www.psychologytoday.com. https://www.psychologytoday.com/us/blog/the-clarity/202109/the-subtle-dance-eye-contact-in-conversation#:~:text=Research%20finds%20that%20direct%20gaze

Turn Your Words into Gold. (n.d.). Love and Logic Institute, Inc. Retrieved January 3, 2023, from https://www.loveandlogic.com/pages/turn-your-word-into-gold

Uono, S., & Hietanen, J. K. (2015). Eye contact perception in the west and east: A cross-cultural study. *PLOS ONE, 10*(2). https://doi.org/10.1371/journal.pone.0118094

Winerman, L. (2005, October). The mind's mirror. *Https://Www.apa.org.* https://www.apa.org/monitor/oct05/mirror

About the Authors

Erika Bare has been a proud educator for over twenty years, serving in a variety of roles. She currently serves as the Assistant Superintendent for the Ashland School District in beautiful Southern Oregon. She grew up in Portland, OR, graduating from the University of Oregon with a Master's in Education in 2001. She dove headfirst into her career as a special education teacher at the middle school level, thriving as both a resource teacher and self-contained teacher. In this work, she endeavored to provide each student with the individualized supports needed to reach their limitless potential. This continued to inspire her when her family relocated to Southern Oregon, and she became a special education teacher on special assignment serving K-12 students.

She earned her administrative credential in 2012 at Southern Oregon University, and transitioned to an administrative role at award winning Ashland High School as assistant principal and then principal. She had the great privilege of teaching and learning alongside a tremendous group of educators for seven joy-filled years. Following a desire to work with our youngest students, she moved to the elementary level as principal in a neighboring district, before being called to have a broader impact at the district office level. She now oversees special education, counseling and behavioral health, social emotional learning, and elementary programs. Supporting all students through individualized supports continues to fuel her today, serving as both her why and her passion.

Erika lives in Southern Oregon with her extremely supportive husband, two remarkable high school aged children, and a very mischievous cat. She feels especially fortunate to live in the community she serves. Erika has developed and led workshops and professional development activities addressing a multitude of topics in education, communication, equity, and leadership. Connect with Erika at connectingthroughconversation.com or email her at: info@connectingthroughconversation.com.

Tiffany Burns lives in the Siskiyou Mountains outside Ashland, Oregon with her college sweetheart husband and their two fabulous children. Her house is a hub of activity–always full of kids, friends, family, and pets.

Tiffany appreciates that working with kids is an art and a science and earned both a Master of Arts in Teaching and a Master of Science in Education, along with endorsements in administration and teaching English to Speakers of Other Languages at Southern Oregon University. In her two decades in education, she taught elementary, middle, high school, and university students in public, private, bilingual, and homeschool settings in Oregon, Alaska, and Mexico. She has served as an instructional and extracurricular coach, curriculum writer and consultant, and creator and facilitator of workshops and professional development in education, equity, leadership, and communication.

Tiffany has been a school administrator since 2012. She is currently the principal of a wonderful elementary school—which she finds to be simultaneously the most rewarding and bizarre job she's held to date. Connect with Tiffany at connectingthroughconversation.com or email her at: info@connectingthroughconversation.com.

Acknowledgements

Creating something that will be meaningful and important in supporting our students takes a tremendous amount of time and energy, and these sacrifices do not rest with the authors alone. This is especially true of our spouses and children who supported us, making sacrifices of time and attention as we dove headfirst into this project.

We are endlessly grateful to Alec Dickinson, Tiffany's husband, for the illustrations and his willingness to read, edit, and provide feedback on a seemingly constant loop throughout the writing process. Additionally, we would like to offer a huge thank you to Erika's parents for providing us a beautiful space by the ocean to provide the inspiration and quiet needed to create this work. We deeply appreciate Tyler Bare, Erika's husband, for his patience in keeping us on track with the behind-the-scenes part of this work. None of this would be possible without the phenomenal educators who talk with kids in the Ashland School District. The tremendous expertise freely shared, the collegial support, and the continued dedication to serve the whole child is beyond compare. We are especially grateful to Michelle Cummings and Steve Retzlaff who were mentors and models as we began our administrative journey. Thank you does not feel big enough to express how grateful we are for the privilege of serving alongside all of our administrative colleagues, past and present, who taught us so much.

Erika would like to thank her parents for their modeling of public service, and particularly her mom's modeling of what it is to be a connected educator and mom. She is grateful to her brother and sister, who allowed her to practice school on an endless loop growing up, and how clear they were when she got it wrong (and occasionally right). She cannot imagine navigating life without the support of her long-time crew: Elizabeth, Shannon, Cindy, and Jill. Finally, to the educators of Athey Creek, Medford Student Services, Griffen Creek, and of course, Ashland High School, she is so grateful to have grown and learned alongside you.

Tiffany would like to thank her family: mom, sister, grandma, and in-laws for their love and modeling of hard work and dedication. She is also grateful to her besties: Molly, Tara, Lindsey, and Aleta for their unwavering belief and support; Matthew Reynolds for helping her to craft her equity lens; Kate Sullivan for her curious questions; Jean Roorda, Sharon Kraus, and Nando Raynolds for their inspiration; and the Walker Wolf Pack for allowing her to learn, grow, and howl beside them.

There are too many colleagues and friends who have supported us in this project to name each and every one of you. To those who read early versions of our manuscript and provided your brilliant insights and ideas, you made this work stronger. We are so grateful. Many of our friends and colleagues served as cheerleaders, and their support kept us going, especially when we weren't sure we wanted to. Thank you.

Finally, we so appreciate ConnectEDD for their belief in our work, as well as their dedication and support to make it great.

More from
ConnectEDD Publishing

Since 2015, ConnectEDD has worked to transform education by empowering educators to become better-equipped to teach, learn, and lead. What started as a small company designed to provide professional learning events for educators has grown to include a variety of services to help educators and administrators address essential challenges. ConnectEDD offers instructional and leadership coaching, professional development workshops focusing on a variety of educational topics, a roster of nationally recognized educator associates who possess hands-on knowledge and experience, educational conferences custom-designed to meet the specific needs of schools, districts, and state/national organizations, and ongoing, personalized support, both virtually and onsite. In 2020, ConnectEDD expanded to include publishing services designed to provide busy educators with books and resources consisting of practical information on a wide variety of teaching, learning, and leadership topics. Please visit us online at connecteddpublishing.com or contact us at: info@connecteddpublishing.com

Recent Publications:

Live Your Excellence: Action Guide by Jimmy Casas

Culturize: Action Guide by Jimmy Casas

Daily Inspiration for Educators: Positive Thoughts for Every Day of the Year by Jimmy Casas

Eyes on Culture: Multiply Excellence in Your School by Emily Paschall

Pause. Breathe. Flourish. Living Your Best Life as an Educator by William D. Parker

L.E.A.R.N.E.R. Finding the True, Good, and Beautiful in Education by Marita Diffenbaugh

Educator Reflection Tips Volume II: Refining Our Practice by Jami Fowler-White

Handle With Care: Managing Difficult Situations in Schools with Dignity and *Respect* by Jimmy Casas and Joy Kelly

Disruptive Thinking: Preparing Learners for Their Future by Eric Sheninger

Permission to be Great: Increasing Engagement in Your School by Dan Butler

Daily Inspiration for Educators: Positive Thoughts for Every Day of the Year, *Volume II* by Jimmy Casas

The 6 Literacy Levers: Creating a Community of Readers by Brad Gustafson

The Educator's ATLAS: Your Roadmap to Engagement by Weston Kieschnick

In This Season: Words for the Heart by Todd Nesloney, LaNesha Tabb, Tanner Olson, and Alice Lee

Leading with a Humble Heart: A 40-Day Devotional for Leaders by Zac Bauermaster

Recalibrate the Culture: Our Why…Our Work…Our Values by Jimmy Casas

Creating Curious Classrooms: The Beauty of Questions by Emma Chiappetta

Crafting the Culture: 45 Reflections on What Matters Most by Joe Sanfelippo and Jeffrey Zoul

Improving School Mental Health: The Thriving School Community Solution by Charle Peck and Dr. Cameron Caswell

Building Authenticity: A Blueprint for the Leader Inside You by Todd Nesloney and Tyler Cook

37180035R00124